Everyday Blessings

Everyday Blessings

Inspirational words of comfort and hope

Aled Jones

HODDER &
STOUGHTON

First published in Great Britain in 2020 by Hodder & Stoughton
An Hachette UK company

4

Copyright © Aled Jones, 2020
Illustrations © Jerry Hoare

The right of Aled Jones to be identified as the Author of the Work
has been asserted by him in accordance with the
Copyright, Designs and Patents Act 1988.

Unless indicated otherwise, Scripture quotations are taken from the Holy Bible,
New International Version (Anglicised edition). Copyright © 1979, 1984, 2011
by Biblica Inc.® Used by permission. All rights reserved.

Extract on 11 April taken from the song 'In Christ Alone' by Stuart Townend
© Thankyou Music Adm. by Capitol CMG Publishing worldwide excl.
UK & Europe, admin by Integrity Music, part of the David C Cook family,
songs@integritymusic.com

Extract on 26 May © Elizabeth Gilbert, EAT PRAY LOVE, 2010,
Bloomsbury Publishing Plc.

Extract on 10 July © Andrew Chinn, 2017. Used with permission.

Every reasonable effort has been made to trace copyright holders, but if
there are any errors or omissions, Hodder & Stoughton will be pleased to insert
the appropriate acknowledgement in any subsequent printings or editions.

A CIP catalogue record for this title is available from the British Library

Hardback ISBN 978 1 473 68274 0
eBook ISBN 978 1 473 68275 7

Printed and bound in Great Britain by Clays Ltd, Elcograf S.p.A.

Hodder & Stoughton policy is to use papers that are natural, renewable
and recyclable products and made from wood grown in sustainable forests.
The logging and manufacturing processes are expected to conform to
the environmental regulations of the country of origin.

Hodder & Stoughton Ltd
Carmelite House
50 Victoria Embankment
London EC4Y 0DZ

www.hodderfaith.com

To Emilia and Lucas
with all my heart

JULY
Childhood Memories

AUGUST
The Arts

SEPTEMBER
Back to School

OCTOBER
Conkers!

NOVEMBER
Remembrance

DECEMBER
The Most Wonderful
Time of the Year

Introduction

Everyday Blessings is to be used and enjoyed by those who follow a particular faith and those who don't. You see, whether you're Christian, Hindu, Jewish, Buddhist, Muslim, Quaker, Mormon, Baha'i, Jehovah's Witness, Agnostic, Pagan or Undecided, there is much to be gained by the words contained in this book. (Apologies if I didn't list your particular persuasion there, but what I'm trying to get across is that this book is for . . . everyone!)

Over the many years I've been presenting religious programmes for television and radio, I've spent countless hours with all sorts of people, of various faith backgrounds, and plenty of non-believers too. And I've come to realise first hand that, basically, we're all the same. So surely people of all faiths and none should be able to live, work and play together? Perhaps you think this a simplistic or even naive view, especially when you watch the news and see people harming each other time and time again in the name of 'their' God. But that is the antithesis of what God stands for as far as I'm concerned, and I firmly believe that, in those situations, 'God' is not on the side of those doing the harming and killing; what we are seeing is a woeful failure within the human spirit to embrace one another and our experiences of the world.

A lot has been made about the conflict between different faiths for centuries; indeed, 'faith' is seen as the root of all evil by some, even in the present day. We're all entitled to our opinion, and I've been on the receiving end of many of these 'opinions' myself. Only recently, when I presented the flagship BBC Radio 2 Sunday morning spiritual show, I was seriously taken aback by some of the messages that came in from so-called 'people of faith' – people who showed no tolerance, or more importantly, love and empathy for those not of their ilk. One email which has stuck with me read as follows: 'How dare you have that Muslim on the show. Yours, through Christ . . .'. Err, hang on for just a moment! Have you forgotten what Christ is all about?! Equally, I've lost track of the times I've been called a 'God-bothering choirboy' by those who clearly don't go to church! Nevertheless, I still trust that these negative voices are a minority. After all, we are all cut from the same cloth; we just end up becoming different garments. And, believe it or not, not all my friends are Christians but are a real mixed bag (apologies for that description, dear friends). For the record, most are agnostic. But they're all really great people, with kind hearts and a wicked sense of humour.

At the core of each and every faith is love. And even if we are of no faith, we are still programmed deep down to be compassionate and to care for our fellow humans and all of creation. Sometimes we can forget that – and how those who kill in the name of faith can actually be religious, I just don't know. To me, it simply doesn't add up. Our shared humanity can certainly seem under threat at times and perhaps a mixture of our pressured modern society and age-old hubris can cause us to lose track of what faith is all about. That is why it was vital for me to group all these blessings together. If you're even vaguely spiritual then kind-heartedness will be at the centre of your being (unless, of course, you're being trolled on social media, when all bets are off!). We can and all should live together in harmony.

I hope too that this collection may serve as something of an antidote to another aspect of our twenty-first century life that is having detrimental effects on our well-being. We live in a world that has so many options available to us. Today, when you turn on the television, for instance, you are confronted by hundreds of channels as opposed to three when I was a child. Nowadays, it's all about the subscription package to the latest streaming service – anything is available for a small monthly fee, and our natural human greed wants to have it all, at a cost which may be out of our reach. So, we stick it on credit and therein starts a vicious circle. It's hard to resist the temptation to have what we want exactly when we want it, 'on demand', as the saying goes.

Not only has consumerism burgeoned over the last few decades but also the sheer pace of life has accelerated so much, becoming faster than ever before. Our unrelenting world consistently invites us to step on the fast track and once you're on that track it seems impossible not to *feel* rushed, busy, stressed and generally overwhelmed. The modern world, it seems, urges us to be everywhere and do everything . . . *all of the time*. The bar is set sky-high. A young friend of mine told me recently that it's all about being 'relevant'. (I tried to point out that I'd never really been 'relevant', except for a brief period in 1985 when I sang 'Walking in the Air'.) But I am of the view that you can't be relevant all of the time. Life is a marathon not a sprint. Slow down to achieve more, that's what I say. Slow down to stay relevant!

So the idea of this compendium is to do just that, to help you *slow down* and take stock of your life situation. I hope you will feel able to take a moment at the start of each day, or whenever time allows, just to sit back and simply exist. Don't try to be relevant! Take in the words on the page and make *them* relevant to *you*. You'll notice that, throughout the book, there is journalling space for you to use as you will. The blessings might inspire the poet in you to come out, or they may even motivate you to draw something. Please use these spaces for whatever you want, even if it's a last-minute rushed shopping list!

The world has changed so much due to the Coronavirus pandemic and everyone has suffered in some way – some much more than others. I hope the words of wisdom in this book transport you somewhere else and offer comfort and hope in equal measure. Whether you believe in God and subscribe to a particular faith or simply want to reconnect with our shared humanity across the ages, these blessings and inspirational thoughts are just the tonic. And you don't need gin and a slice to make them more palatable! Cheers!

New Beginnings

The writer Mark Twain, regarded by many as the father of American literature, was sceptical about the resolutions we all make at this time of year. He wrote: 'Now is the accepted time to make your regular annual good resolutions. Next week you can begin paving hell with them as usual.' But modern-day self-help gurus certainly would have us believe that January is a new start – the month of new beginnings. Hence the overcrowded gyms with over-indulgers vowing that *this* is the year they get that perfect body.

For me, it is quite the opposite; I'm with Mr Twain! I find January, for the most part, quite hellish. It's a cold, miserable and dark stretch after the warmth of the heartening Christmas season. Gone are the multicoloured fairylights, bright tinsel and festive wrapping paper. Gone are the gladdening carols and the feel-good spirit. Instead, all you see through the freezing mist and torrential rain are mountains of discarded Christmas trees tossed into roads and bins, now forgotten and insignificant, when previously they stood proud and important – beckoning families and communities together. It's almost as if Big Ben bongs and everything changes. Cold, deflated reality sets in, and I know that, within minutes, I'll be biting my nails once again, even though I did have every intention of quitting (I have had the same resolution since I was a child. There's always next year, eh?).

January, if crooner Fred Astaire is to be believed, is a time to pick yourself up (literally off the floor for some!), dust yourself off and start all over again. And therein lies one of the problems for me: I don't want to start again from scratch, thank you very much. I love the end-of-year warm feeling of contentment. Why can't it be Christmas all year round? I remember asking my parents the very same question as a six-year-old, probably having just watched *Songs of Praise* on TV, only for my dad to say, matter-of-factly: 'It can't, I'm afraid. Now get in the bath, it's school tomorrow.' Oh, the down-to-earth trauma of it. (It does sound slightly less traumatic spoken in Welsh though!)

Maybe that's the defining moment from my childhood when my intense dislike for January began. You see, I like everything to be nice and shiny in my world. I like it when everyone is happy, even if it is, in part, only down to too much sherry. Let's face it, there's no making merry in January. It's a time of harsh realities and intense struggles with 'dryness'. It is an empty month when my diary is mostly blank. The social calendar is a thing of the past, the days seem to drag on and on indefinitely and the nights are long. I spend time flicking through photos on Instagram of those fortunate enough to be strolling along that picture-perfect beach in the Maldives or lying on a sun lounger next to a so-called celeb at the Sandy Lane Resort in Barbados.

By now you're probably thinking, 'My goodness, Aled, you really don't like January, do you? Come on lad, it's not that bad!' But hold the front page, all is not lost: you'll be pleased to hear I've come to the conclusion that there *is* some light in the darkness.

January's only redeeming feature for me comes courtesy of my bichon dog Cybi, the fluffiest pick-me-up ever. For eleven years he was my saving grace. The wag of his tail would mean 'walkies' and off we'd go on a wintry adventure together. I'm very fortunate that my singing career takes me all over the world and, more often than not, I end up in much warmer climes than good ol' Blighty during the year. But I wouldn't have missed those crisp January strolls for anything. They were so soul-enhancing and certainly lifted me out of the New Year bleakness. It was just me and my best friend, experiencing the breaking of the new day before the majority of the rest of the world began to stir – a real bonding experience and one that I cherished. And I think he loved it too, judging by the amount of time he would take savouring each and every smell. Picture the scene if you can: a walking, white, soft, fleecy cloud, with warm steam rising from his button-black nose, as he sniffs with delight the fresh, untouched, dewy grass. A very special moment, 'frozen' (literally!) in time.

But last year the heart and soul of our family left us for doggy heaven. Cybi had been right at the centre of our lives. He was our everything and his passing devastated us all to the core. To say that we adored him is a huge understatement. He was such a gentle soul who, even in times of adversity – of which there were many – never gave up and never showed any moments of self-pity. In his precious, simple world, January was just like every other month, offering up abundant opportunities for adventure and fun.

Bearing all that in mind, the good resolution that I'm sticking to this year – and ever more – is to keep Cybi's positive, kind, indomitable spirit well and truly alive, and to strive daily to be more like him. Whatever life threw at him he would pick himself up, dust himself off and start all over again.

So, deep breath everyone, cheers to the New Year! It might not be plain sailing but let's go for it! Let's start all over again with joy in our January hearts. Let's do it for Cybi.

1 January

Hold on to what is good,
Even if it's a handful of earth.
Hold on to what you believe,
Even if it's a tree that stands by itself.
Hold on to what you must do,
Even if it's a long way from here.
Hold on to your life,
Even if it's easier to let go.
Hold on to my hand,
Even if someday I'll be gone away from you.

A PUEBLO INDIAN PRAYER

2 January

Would you like me to give you a
formula for success? It's quite simple,
really. Double your rate of failure. You
are thinking of failure as the enemy of
success. But it isn't at all. You can be
discouraged by failure or you can learn
from it, so go ahead and make mistakes.
Make all you can. Because remember
that's where you will find success.

THOMAS J. WATSON

3 January

I count my blessings as follows:

1. I'm alive.
2. Beauty is in the world all around me.
3. I share my love with everyone and not just a select few.
4. I give thanks to whoever made and created us no matter which religion it may be.
5. I never stop smiling, laughing and being happy.
6. I try to help those who need it the most.
7. I try not to hate, injure or kill anything or anyone.
8. I share what I have even if I don't have much.
9. I write and share my thoughts so that it may bring comfort to other people.
10. I never ask for anything for me from anyone.
11. I follow the other ten blessings.

ANTHONY T. HINCKS

4 January

The best preparation for tomorrow
is doing your best today.

H. JACKSON BROWN, JR

5 January

When you were born, you cried
And the world rejoiced.
Live your life
So that when you die,
The world cries and you rejoice.

CHEROKEE PROVERB

6 January

I know you're tired. The year just
began and yet you already feel restless
and sometimes weak, but you must
never forget that you were always
meant to survive. You must always
remember that you are more powerful
than the anything or anyone who
wants to destroy you.

R.H. SIN

7 January

Fortune befriends the bold.

EMILY DICKINSON

8 January

May the road rise to meet you.
May the wind be ever at you back.
May the sun shine warm upon your face;
The rain fall soft upon your fields
And until we meet again,
May God hold you, may God hold you
Ever in the palm of His hand.

IRISH BLESSING

9 January

Be happy for this moment.
This moment is your life.

OMAR KHAYYAM

10 January

Today I choose life. Every morning when I wake up I can choose joy, happiness, negativity, pain . . . To feel the freedom that comes from being able to continue to make mistakes and choices – today I choose to feel life, not to deny my humanity but embrace it.

KEVYN AUCOIN

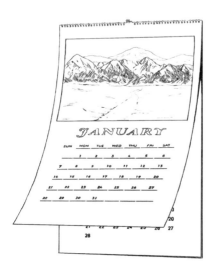

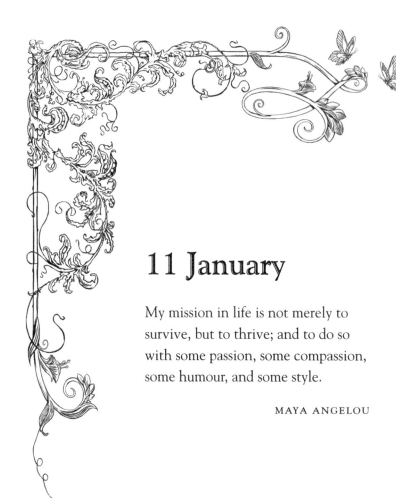

11 January

My mission in life is not merely to survive, but to thrive; and to do so with some passion, some compassion, some humour, and some style.

MAYA ANGELOU

12 January

Permanence, perseverance and persistence
in spite of all obstacles, discouragements,
and impossibilities: it is this, that in all things
distinguishes the strong soul from the weak.

THOMAS CARLYLE

13 January

All our dreams can come true, if we have the
courage to pursue them.

WALT DISNEY

14 January

The secret of change is to focus all of your energy not on fighting the old, but on building the new.

DAN MILLMAN

15 January

There may be a long list of things to do, but really, there is just one thing on the list at any time. If you think of it like that, the whole world looks different and you can stay quite calm. Maybe everything will get done eventually and maybe not. You can always have hope.

ZOKETSU NORMAN FISCHER

16 January

The only person you are destined to become is the person you decide to be.

RALPH WALDO EMERSON

17 January

Let us make our future now, and let us make our dreams tomorrow's reality.

MALALA YOUSAFZAI

18 January

Nothing is impossible. The word itself says, 'I'm possible!'

AUDREY HEPBURN

19 January

You don't always need a plan.
Sometimes you just need to breathe,
trust, let go, and see what happens.

MANDY HALE

20 January

Life can only be understood backwards;
but it must be lived forwards.

SØREN KIERKEGAARD

21 January

Don't think, just do.

HORACE

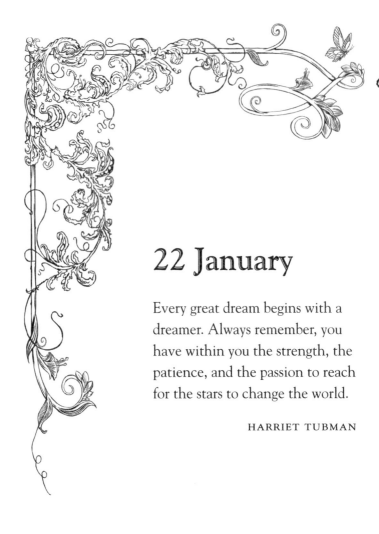

22 January

Every great dream begins with a dreamer. Always remember, you have within you the strength, the patience, and the passion to reach for the stars to change the world.

HARRIET TUBMAN

23 January

It's a wise man who understands that every day is
a new beginning, because, boy, how many mistakes
do you make in a day? I don't know about you, but
I make plenty. You can't turn the clock back, so you
have to look ahead.

MEL GIBSON

24 January

Optimism is the faith that leads to achievement.
Nothing can be done without hope and confidence.

HELEN KELLER

25 January

Only I can change my life. No one can do it for me.

CAROL BURNETT

26 January

There is no passion to be found playing small – in settling for a life that is less than the one you are capable of living.

NELSON MANDELA

27 January

Don't think about what can happen in a month. Don't think about what can happen in a year. Just focus on the twenty-four hours in front of you and do what you can to get closer to where you want to be.

ERIC THOMAS

28 January

Your time is limited, so don't waste it living someone else's life. Don't be trapped by dogma – which is living with the results of other people's thinking. Don't let the noise of others' opinions drown out your own inner voice. And most important, have the courage to follow your heart and intuition.

STEVE JOBS

29 January

Pursue some path, however narrow
and crooked, in which you can walk
with love and reverence.

HENRY DAVID THOREAU

30 January

Your attitude, not your aptitude,
will determine your altitude.

ZIG ZIGLAR

31 January

Every day brings new choices.

MARTHA BECK

Love Never Fails

February is the month of love, when our thoughts turn to romance. Just don't forget Valentine's Day, whatever you do! If the day itself falls on a Sunday, when my Classic FM show is broadcast, I get so many desperate emails dropping into my inbox from forgetful partners: 'Please, Aled, say "I love you" to the love of my life!' I mean, I try my best to help, but can't honour every single request. I'm not Cupid after all, just some bloke on the radio. And maybe said love of your life would rather hear those loving words from the horse's mouth? I'd hazard a guess that a verbal proclamation of love spoken directly from you would go down much better; I dare say too that such a proclamation would be far more appreciated than some dodgy-looking flowers purchased in haste at the local garage!

Now, I don't want you to think that I'm not romantic, because I am (I try to be romantic every day of the year, you see, not just on one day!). But for me the attraction of Valentine's Day has diminished over the years. I used to get very excited about this day of love when I was at school. We boys would talk about who we were going to send our cards to, with the obligatory question mark as a signature, for weeks before the big day and, needless to say, it became a competition as to who could receive the most cards. I did very well one year when I got five – only to find out later that they had all come from my family!

I remember one Valentine's Day from this period very clearly. I was keen on a girl from a neighbouring school and had a tiny inkling that she didn't regard me as a total loser choirboy (which many did!). On the day itself our two schools were playing a football match and as I ran on to the pitch it happened: *she* personally handed *me* a card, clearly not wanting any element of surprise. She had signed the card H-L-N . . . and, guess what, her name was Helen! Still, it was a lovely thought, and I was delighted to receive the card, even though there was absolutely no doubt as to who it was from!

What, then, is love? Is it what we see on the Spanish shores of ITV2's *Love Island*? Or is it what Shakespeare described in his play *Love's Labour's Lost*?

When Love speaks, the voice of all the gods
Makes heaven drowsy with the harmony.

I've been very fortunate because I've experienced unconditional love throughout my life and I now have my own loving family. Growing up in North Wales, I was encased in the warm and protective love I received from my parents and grandparents who adored me. And, indeed, the devotion I now feel towards my own children is the ultimate, unadulterated love.

I'm also blessed to have a deep love for music. Even when I was a toddler, I had within me this huge desire to sing. I would harmonise with anything and everything, from songs on the radio to the sound made by running water or even the hairdryer (please tell me other people make up songs when drying their hair!). The love I feel for music – and singing in particular – has only grown and deepened over the years. I'm often asked in interviews how I would have felt had I not had a good enough voice to sing, after my voice broke. My answer is always the same: I knew I'd sing again. Whether in the Royal Albert Hall or just in the shower wasn't up to me. As long as I sang, I'd be all right. Thankfully, I've been lucky enough to continue a wonderfully happy love affair with singing, an affair I've conducted in the Albert Hall and many other places! And long may it continue.

But back to Valentine's Day. What's it all about? Is it really about chocolates, flowers, red hearts and romance? The origins of the day aren't traditionally romantic at all. There are many legends surrounding Saint Valentine. He was probably a Roman priest in the third century AD, when Christians were being persecuted by the Emperor Claudius, who had established an order prohibiting young people from getting married. By all accounts, this was based on the supposition that unmarried soldiers fought better than married ones, because married soldiers might fear what would happen to their wives or families if they died in battle. Valentine went behind the emperor's back and secretly married young couples; but he was eventually caught, imprisoned and tortured for performing marriage ceremonies against the command of the emperor.

There are plenty of myths about Valentine's time in prison. One of the men who was judging him in line with the Roman law at the time was a ruthless man called Asterius, whose daughter Julia was blind. Valentine is said to have restored her sight by praying to God while laying his hands on her eyes. Asterius became a Christian as a result. Nevertheless, later on, in AD 269 Valentine was caught again and sentenced to a three-part execution by beating, stoning and, finally, decapitation, all because of his association with Christian marriage. The legend goes that the last words he wrote were in a note to Asterius' daughter, instigating what has now become the norm by signing it, 'from your Valentine'.

When it comes to love it's not all about Saint Valentine, though. We Welsh have our very own patron saint of love, who is celebrated at the end of January. Her story is just as fanciful as Valentine's and dates back to the fifth century. She's called Dwynwen and was the prettiest of King Brychan Brycheiniog's twenty-four daughters. (The king was obviously very much in love, judging by the numbers!) Dwynwen fell head over heels with a local boy called Maelon Dafodrill, but King Brychan had already arranged for her to marry a prince. Maelon took the news badly, as you would imagine, and the equally distressed Dwynwen fled to the woods to weep, begging God to help her. She was visited by an angel who gave her a sweet potion to take so that she would forget Maelon, which in turn transformed him into a block of ice (don't you just hate it when that happens?!).

God granted Dwynwen three wishes. Her first was that Maelon be thawed; her second that God help all true lovers everywhere; and her third was that she would never marry. She showed her gratefulness to God for granting these wishes by becoming a nun and set up a convent on Llanddwyn Island, one of my favourite places on earth and near my home on Anglesey in North Wales. Dwynwen's name means 'she who leads a blessed life' and I certainly feel blessed whenever I visit Llanddwyn Island. It is an idyllic spot, where the remains of Dwynwen's church can still be seen today.

So, if you wish to make your romantic feelings *really* known to a loved one, then why not have two bites at the cherry? Go with 'dwi'n dy garu di' at the end of January for Saint Dwynwen's Day and 'I love you' three weeks later for Saint Valentine's Day! Surely that should seal the deal in a much more romantic fashion than if you left it in the hands of that bloke on the radio!

1 February

Where there is love there is life.

MAHATMA GANDHI

2 February

Never apologise for showing feeling.
When you do so, you apologise for the truth.

BENJAMIN DISRAELI

3 February

When the power of love overcomes the love of power, the world will know peace.

JIMI HENDRIX

4 February

The best and most beautiful things in the world cannot be seen or even touched – they must be felt with the heart.

HELEN KELLER

5 February

Spread love everywhere you go.
Let no one ever come to you without
leaving happier.

MOTHER TERESA

6 February

Love yourself. It is important to stay positive because beauty comes from the inside out.

JENN PROSKE

7 February

I fall in love every day. Not with people
but with situations.

AMY WINEHOUSE

8 February

Love all, trust a few, do wrong to none.

WILLIAM SHAKESPEARE

9 February

Infuse your life with action. Don't wait for it to happen.
Make it happen. Make your own future. Make your own
hope. Make your own love. And whatever your beliefs,
honour your creator, not by passively waiting for grace
to come down from upon high, but by doing what you
can to make grace happen . . . yourself, right now, right
down here on earth.

BRADLEY WHITFORD

10 February

When you wish someone joy, you
wish them peace, love, prosperity,
happiness . . . all the good things.

MAYA ANGELOU

11 February

Love myself I do. Not everything, but I love the good as well as the bad. I love my crazy lifestyle, and I love my hard discipline. I love my freedom of speech and the way my eyes get dark when I'm tired. I love that I have learned to trust people with my heart, even if it will get broken. I am proud of everything that I am and will become.

JOHNNY WEIR

12 February

The pain of parting is nothing
to the joy of meeting again.

CHARLES DICKENS

13 February

It is easy to hate and it is difficult to love. This is how the whole scheme of things works. All good things are difficult to achieve; and bad things are very easy to get.

CONFUCIUS

14 February

Sometimes you have to step away from what you love in order to learn how to love it again.

DAMIEN RICE

15 February

You can't stay in your corner of the forest
waiting for others to come to you. You have
to go to them sometimes.

A.A. MILNE

16 February

But let there be spaces in your togetherness
and let the winds of the heavens dance
between you. Love one another but make
not a bond of love: let it rather be a moving
sea between the shores of your souls.

KHALIL GIBRAN

17 February

Love yourself first and everything else falls into line. You really have to love yourself to get anything done in this world.

LUCILLE BALL

18 February

A friend is someone who knows all about you and still loves you.

ELBERT HUBBARD

19 February

I believe that imagination is stronger than knowledge.
That myth is more potent than history. That dreams are
more powerful than facts. That hope always triumphs
over experience. That laughter is the only cure for grief.
And I believe that love is stronger than death.

ROBERT FULGHUM

20 February

'Tis better to have loved and lost
Than never to have loved at all.

ALFRED, LORD TENNYSON

21 February

Be loving towards yourself, then you
will be able to love others too.

OSHO

22 February

In the sweetness of friendship let there
be laughter, and sharing of pleasures.
For in the dew of little things the heart
finds its morning and is refreshed.

KHALIL GIBRAN

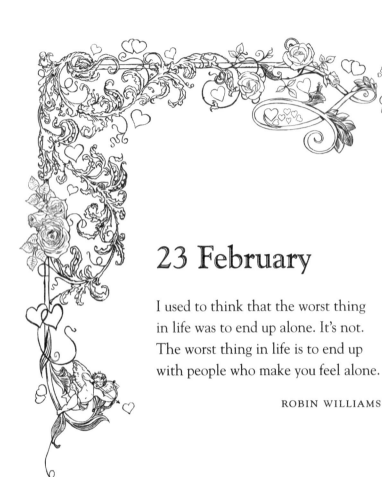

23 February

I used to think that the worst thing
in life was to end up alone. It's not.
The worst thing in life is to end up
with people who make you feel alone.

ROBIN WILLIAMS

24 February

When you meet the one who changes the way your heart beats, dance with them to that rhythm for as long as the song lasts.

KIRK DIEDRICH

25 February

But every house where Love abides
And Friendship is a guest,
Is surely home, and home, sweet home,
For there the hearts can rest.

HENRY VAN DYKE

26 February

Oh, the comfort, the inexpressible comfort
of feeling safe with a person, having neither to
weigh thoughts, nor measure words, but pouring
them all out, just as they are, chaff and grain
together; knowing that a faithful hand will take
and sift them – keep what is worth keeping – and
with the breath of kindness blow the rest away.

DINAH CRAIK

27 February

The secret to living well and longer is:
eat half, walk double, laugh triple and
love without measure.

TIBETAN PROVERB

28 February

Life has taught us that love does not
consist in gazing at each other but in
looking together in the same direction.

ANTOINE DE SAINT-EXUPÉRY

29 February

All the windows of my heart
I open to the day.

JOHN GREENLEAF WHITTIER

Do the Little Things

The first day of March is a very important day in the Welsh calendar. It's when we celebrate our patron saint, David. As young children in school we would wear a daffodil or leek in his honour and sing songs about him being ever-such-a-good man, which you would generally expect from your patron saint, wouldn't you (although a priest friend of mine with a big sense of humour once remarked that saints are only sinners who've been edited!).

So why choose the daffodil and leek as national emblems? The daffodil is a relatively new addition, but the tradition of the leek as a symbol of Wales and all things Welsh is so old that the origins are, by now, lost in time. It is highly likely that it goes back to the days of the druids, the priests who controlled society in the centuries before the Romans came to Britain. In those pagan times, people worshipped trees, plants and flowers and saw magical properties within them, believing them to be sacred. The leek was revered as something that could not only help cure colds and alleviate the pains of childbirth, but also be used to keep away evil spirits and to see into the future. (This is the main reason I have them growing in abundance on my allotment!) One common belief was that a young girl who put leeks beneath her pillow at night would see the face of her future husband in her dreams. Just imagine the smell though! No doubt, said husband always went by the name 'Pugh'!

Enough about leeks, let's get back to Saint David. He was born in the mid-sixth century and, according to legend, his mother Saint Non gave birth to him on a Pembrokeshire clifftop during a fierce storm. If you visit, you'll see the exact spot marked by the ruins of Non's chapel alongside a nearby holy well that is said to have healing powers. I filmed a programme there once and, upon arrival, found that a pilgrim, obviously suffering, had used it as a toilet – not the restorative experience I was hoping for!

David became a renowned preacher, founding monastic settlements and churches in Wales, Brittany and south-west England, including, possibly, the abbey at Glastonbury. David and his monks followed a very simple, austere life, ploughing the fields and carrying their tools by hand, rather than using animals. They also refrained from eating meat or drinking beer. Saint David himself was reputed to have consumed only herbs, bread and water. His most famous miracle took place when he was preaching to a large crowd in Llanddewi Brefi. When people at the back complained that they could not hear him, the ground on which he stood rose up to form a hill. A white dove, sent by God, settled on his shoulder. Now that's what you call a miracle!

David died on 1 March AD 589 and it is said that the monastery 'filled with angels as Christ received his soul'. The place where he was buried became a popular place of pilgrimage throughout the Middle Ages and St David's cathedral now stands on that site. Four visits to St David's were considered the equivalent of two to Rome, and one to Jerusalem. His last words to his followers came from a sermon he gave before his death: 'Be joyful and keep your faith and your creed. Do the little things that you have seen me do and heard about.' The phrase 'Gwnewch y pethau bychain mewn bywyd', 'Do the little things in life', is still a well-known adage in Wales. And it's this that I will endeavour to cling on to this month, enjoying and making the most of what I have right in front of me. In this fast-moving age of social media it's very easy to get caught up in others' lives and others' belongings, to strive for what is out of our reach.

(It was the other great Welsh 'saint', Tom Jones, who told us wisely to focus on the green, green grass of home after all. And I always try to do what 'Saint Tom' tells me!) It's not always possible to keep up with the Joneses, you see, even if you are a Jones yourself. Instead, I'm going to try and focus on what is nurturing and sustaining in my life. I am going to strive to show gratitude for those 'little', everyday things that I have possibly started to take for granted.

I remember as a child visiting my nain and taid (gran and grandad in Welsh) and wanting money to go to the local shop. As an impetuous young kid I was only interested in the big bucks. Nain came out with the phrase, 'Look after the pennies, Aled, and the pounds will look after themselves.' I had no idea what she meant until many years afterwards. The former Archbishop of Canterbury (and, before that, Archbishop of Wales), Rowan Williams, believes the phrase 'Do the little things' should, now more than ever, resonate with a modern society: 'It reminds us that the primary things for us are the relationships around us, the need to work at what's under our hands, what's within our reach.' It's vital to show love and care in small, everyday ways, not just to immediate family and friends. It's easy to dismiss the notion that each time we do something that's kind or helpful towards others, it's too small a gesture in the grand scheme of things to make any difference. But I firmly believe that our kind words or loving actions accumulate into something much bigger, just like my nain's pile of pennies.

So, if I pass you on the street and smile at you, or offer up my seat on the bus, please don't think I'm odd. I'm just doing the little things in life. Why not try it too? Let's make March the month of little gestures. Pass it on.

1 March

Be joyful and keep your faith and your creed. Do the little things that you have seen me do and heard about.

ST DAVID

2 March

No amount of blessings can benefit
you if you don't take the first step.

ISRAELMORE AYIVOR

3 March

Do your little bit of good where you are; it's those little bits of good put together that overwhelm the world.

DESMOND TUTU

4 March

Always go to the bathroom when you
have a chance.

KING GEORGE V

5 March

Do all the good you can, by all the
means you can, in all the ways you
can, in all the places you can, at all
the times you can, to all the people
you can, as long as ever you can.

JOHN WESLEY

6 March

Don't count the days,
make the days count.

MUHAMMAD ALI

7 March

The only impossible journey
is the one you never begin.

ANTHONY ROBBINS

8 March

If you cannot do great things,
do small things in a great way.

NAPOLEON HILL

9 March

Vision without action is a daydream.
Action without vision is a nightmare.

10 March

The secret of getting ahead is getting started.

MARK TWAIN

11 March

Do not wait to strike till the iron is hot;
but make it hot by striking.

W.B. YEATS

12 March

Be yourself; everyone else is already taken.

OSCAR WILDE

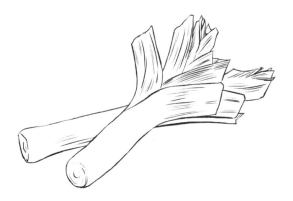

13 March

Don't be afraid to give yourself everything you've ever wanted in life.

ANON

14 March

Good, better, best. Never let it rest.
'Til your good is better and your
better is best.

SAINT JEROME

15 March

I've learned that people will forget what you
said, people will forget what you did, but people
will never forget how you made them feel.

MAYA ANGELOU

16 March

In every day, there are 1,440 minutes.
That means we have 1,440 daily opportunities
to make a positive impact.

LES BROWN

17 March

May you always have work for your hands to do.
May your pockets hold always a coin or two.
May the sun shine bright on your windowpane.
May the rainbow be certain to follow each rain.
May the hand of a friend always be near you.
And may God fill your heart with gladness to cheer you.

18 March

Focus on your strengths, not your weaknesses.
Focus on your character, not your reputation.
Focus on your blessings, not your misfortunes.

ROY T. BENNETT

19 March

Lighten up, just enjoy life, smile more, laugh more, and don't get so worked up about things.

KENNETH BRANAGH

20 March

Saying nothing
sometimes says the most.

EMILY DICKINSON

21 March

If you will not rise above the things
of the world, they will rise above you.

SATHYA SAI BABA

22 March

Have a heart that never hardens, and a temper
that never tires, and a touch that never hurts.

CHARLES DICKENS

23 March

Be sure to put your feet in the right place,
then stand firm.

ABRAHAM LINCOLN

24 March

It does not matter how slowly
you go as long as you do not stop.

CONFUCIUS

25 March

The pessimist sees difficulty in every opportunity. The optimist sees opportunity in every difficulty.

WINSTON CHURCHILL

26 March

Everything you've ever wanted
is on the other side of fear.

GEORGE ADDAIR

27 March

The greatest wealth is to live
content with little.

PLATO

28 March

If you lose hope, somehow you lose the vitality that keeps life moving, you lose that courage to be, the quality that helps you to go on in spite of all. And so today I still have a dream.

MARTIN LUTHER KING, JR

29 March

I had the blues because I had no shoes until
upon the street, I met a man who had no feet.

ANCIENT PERSIAN SAYING

30 March

A grateful heart is a beginning of greatness.
It is an expression of humility. It is a foundation
for the development of such virtues as prayer,
faith, courage, contentment, happiness, love,
and well-being.

JAMES E. FAUST

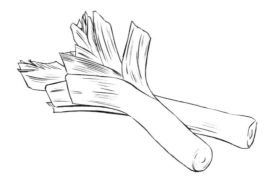

31 March

Have no fear of perfection –
you'll never reach it.

SALVADOR DALI

High Days and Holidays

During the month of April, all the main faiths celebrate important 'feast' days. Let me take us through some of the main ones happening this month.

For Christians, Easter is our most joyous and important festival, commemorating the resurrection of Jesus Christ. However, the most solemn time of the Christian year is Holy Week, the week leading up to Easter, during which Christians remember the last days of Jesus' life. Holy Week begins on Palm Sunday which re-enacts Christ's triumphant arrival in Jerusalem to the cheers of the crowd. Later in the week many of the people in that cheering crowd would be among those shouting for Jesus to be executed. Christian leaders will often use the Palm

Sunday story to help people think about the strength of their own commitment to their faith.

Maundy Thursday is the Thursday of Holy Week, just before Easter, remembered as the day of the Last Supper, when Jesus washed the feet of his disciples and established the ceremony known as the Eucharist (a Christian sacrament in which bread and wine are consecrated and consumed in memory of Jesus' death; the bread and wine symbolise his body and blood). The night of Maundy Thursday is when Judas betrayed Jesus in the Garden of Gethsemane, then, on Good Friday, Jesus was executed by crucifixion. His body was taken down from the cross and buried in a guarded tomb. An enormous stone was put over the entrance, so that no one could steal the body. But after three days, two women disciples of Jesus visited the grave only to find that the stone had been moved and the tomb was empty! Jesus himself was seen that same day, and for days afterwards by many people. His followers realised that God had raised Jesus from the dead.

Now, whether you're a Christian believer or not, you have to admit it's a great story that really does have it all: love, betrayal, hatred, death and resurrection! The magical story and all the ceremony that goes with it is what I loved as a young chorister at Bangor Cathedral. Some of the most uplifting music ever written is performed at Easter and as choristers we really felt we were part of something much bigger than ourselves. We felt an indescribable energy for the whole week. Every service was vital and needed total focus and commitment. Holy Week left you exhausted vocally yet emotionally exhilarated.

A sensation of joy and happiness spreads among Muslims when the month of April or Sha'ban arrives. Sha'ban signals the coming of Ramadan, the best and most blessed month in Islam. Lailat ul Bara'h (Night of Forgiveness) is the fifteenth night of Sha'ban and takes place two weeks before Ramadan. Muslims seek forgiveness for their sins and believe that, on this night, one's destiny is fixed for the year ahead. It is believed that to stand in prayer on this one night is better than a thousand months of worship. Muslims pray and ask God for forgiveness either at the mosque or at home; they may visit the graves of relatives and give to charity. Although not a religious requirement, in some parts of the world there are firework displays that mark this occasion. Muslims believe that their good actions bring a greater reward during Sha'ban than at any other time of year, because it has been blessed by Allah. They also believe that it is easier to do good in this month because the devils have been chained in hell, and the gates of heaven are open. What an amazing vision!

Another term associated with the events and activities of days of sacred significance is 'holy day', from which is derived the word 'holiday'. And on the day of the first full moon in April, one of the three main branches of Buddhism, Theravada (the other two are Mahayana and Vajrayana) celebrates a New Year, with holidays lasting up to a week. April is also the end of the dry season for many South East Asian countries so, perhaps not surprisingly, water features prominently in welcoming in both the New Year as well as the rainy season. Water in Buddhism represents purity and it is used symbolically to 'wash away' one's sins, as well as cleaning homes, statues and temples to welcome in the New Year afresh. You can expect some serious water 'fights' in some countries too!

And there isn't anything quite like a Hindu festival. Larger than life, they tend to seriously catch the eye: bright colours, lavish meals, chanting and even throwing colour sprays at anyone passing have captured the fascination of the world. None more so than at Navratri (literally meaning 'nine nights'), one of the most widely celebrated Hindu festivals. It is celebrated to honour Goddess Durga, who symbolises power and purity. Then there is Rama Navami, the day in April marking the birth of Lord Rama. He is the protagonist of the Ramayana, an epic poem that has vast religious significance in Hinduism. Lord Rama, with his divine prowess and benevolence, slays immoral beings, conquers the realm and establishes order. Hindus observe the festival by giving to charity, holding recitals and attending devotional worship. Many of the faithful also fast for nine days in order to cleanse their bodies.

Spiritual disciplines also play a huge part in the Jewish holiday called Passover. The biblical book of Exodus tells how the Israelites were slaves in Egypt. God visited ten plagues upon the Egyptians to convince Pharaoh to free the Israelites, and during the last of the plagues, the smiting of the first-born sons, God 'passed over' the houses of the Israelites, sparing them his wrath. God parted the Red Sea and the prophet Moses led them to freedom. They wandered through the desert to the Holy Land, and along the way God gave them the Jewish law.

Passover is a celebration of spring, of birth and re-birth, of a journey from slavery to freedom, and of taking responsibility for yourself, the community and the world. The Torah (the law of God handed to Moses) states that Jews are to observe Passover for seven or eight days depending on where they live, beginning on the fifteenth of the Jewish month of Nisan (usually in April). Before celebrations can begin, the house must be cleaned from top to bottom to remove any traces of chametz (leaven) from the home. This commemorates the Jews leaving Egypt who did not have time to let their bread rise, but also symbolises removing 'puffiness' (for which, read arrogance or pride) from their souls.

So April is a pretty busy month when it comes to religious festivals. They teach us about good overcoming evil as well as, in many cases, urging us to fast or purify ourselves in order to gain the most from the impending feast. Quite the opposite to many of us at Christmas time, when too much feasting leads to the inevitable January fasting!

There are some wonderful 'non-religious' festivals happening all over the world too. Since 22 April 1970 we've been marking the anniversary of the birth of the modern environmental movement, known as Earth Day. The day encourages people to think about new ways to reduce their carbon footprint and improve water quality, hold demonstrations to show their support for defences of their environment, and get together to get their hands dirty and take earnest strides towards making the earth a better, and healthier, place to live.

So, as 11 April also marks National Barbershop Quartet Day, let's sing out, put environmental concerns on the front page and positively try to live in harmony together. This is the month to do just that, while cele-brating the spring rebirth. So, wellies on, I'm off to go and splash in some puddles! After all, April showers make way for sweet May flowers.

1 April

'It's impossible', said pride.
'It's risky', said experience.
'It's pointless', said reason.
'Give it a try', whispered the heart.

ANON

2 April

The real voyage of discovery consists not in seeking new lands but seeing with new eyes.

MARCEL PROUST

3 April

The more you praise and celebrate your life,
the more there is in life to celebrate.

OPRAH WINFREY

4 April

Faith is to believe what you do not yet see;
the reward for this faith is to see what you believe.

AUGUSTINE OF HIPPO

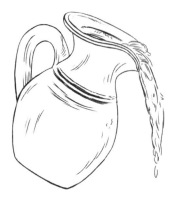

5 April

People usually consider walking on water
or in thin air a miracle. But I think the real
miracle is not to walk either on water or in
thin air, but to walk on earth. Every day we
are engaged in a miracle which we don't even
recognise: a blue sky, white clouds, green
leaves, the black, curious eyes of a child – our
own two eyes. All is a miracle.

THICH NHAT HANH

6 April

Great things never came from comfort zones.

NEIL STRAUSS

7 April

Before God we are all equally wise – and equally foolish.

ALBERT EINSTEIN

8 April

Self-praise is for losers.
Be a winner.
Stand for something.
Always have class,
and be humble.

JOHN MADDEN

9 April

No coward soul is mine,
No trembler in the world's storm-troubled sphere:
I see Heaven's glories shine,
And Faith shines equal, arming me from Fear.

EMILY BRONTË

10 April

Yesterday is history, tomorrow is a mystery,
today is a gift of God, which is why we call it
the present.

BIL KEANE

11 April

No guilt in life, no fear in death.
This is the power of Christ in me;
From life's first cry to final breath,
Jesus commands my destiny.*

STUART TOWNEND

* Extract taken from the song 'In Christ Alone'
by Stuart Townend © Thankyou Music

12 April

Paths are made by walking.

FRANZ KAFKA

13 April

A new command I give you:
Love one another.
As I have loved you,
so you must love one another.

HOLY BIBLE (JOHN 13:34)

14 April

If you don't know where you're going,
any road'll take you there.

GEORGE HARRISON

15 April

The phrase 'Do not be afraid' is written in
the Bible 365 times. That's a daily reminder
from God to live every day being fearless.

ANON

16 April

The most basic and powerful way to connect to another person is to listen. Just listen. Perhaps the most important thing we ever give each other is our attention . . . A loving silence often has far more power to heal and to connect than the most well-intentioned words.

RACHEL NAOMI REMEN

17 April

If there is to be peace in the world,
    there must be peace in the nations.
If there is to be peace in the nations,
    there must be peace in the cities.
If there is to be peace in the cities,
    there must be peace between neighbours.
If there is to be peace between neighbours,
    there must be peace in the home.
If there is to be peace in the home,
    there must be peace in the heart.

LAO TZU

18 April

In the name of God, stop
a moment, cease your work,
look around you.

LEO TOLSTOY

19 April

May God always shower His blessings on you; may He fill your life with hope and may He always guide you on to the right path.

LATIKA TEOTIA

20 April

No one saves us but ourselves.
No one can and no one may.
We ourselves must walk the path.

BUDDHA

21 April

Every birthday is a gift.
Every day is a gift.

ARETHA FRANKLIN

22 April

Earth teach me quiet – as the grasses are still with
   new light.
Earth teach me suffering – as old stones suffer with
   memory.
Earth teach me humility – as blossoms are humble
   with beginning.
Earth teach me caring – as mothers nurture their
   young.
Earth teach me courage – as the tree that stands
   alone.
Earth teach me limitation – as the ant that crawls
   on the ground.
Earth teach me freedom – as the eagle that soars in
   the sky.
Earth teach me acceptance – as the leaves that die
   each fall.
Earth teach me renewal – as the seed that rises in
   the spring.
Earth teach me to forget myself – as melted snow
   forgets its life.
Earth teach me to remember kindness – as dry
   fields weep with rain.

UTE PRAYER

23 April

Now this is not the end. It is not even the beginning of the end. But it is, perhaps, the end of the beginning.

WINSTON CHURCHILL

24 April

Better than a thousand hollow words, is one word that brings peace.

BUDDHA

25 April

I am with you always, to the very end of the age.

HOLY BIBLE (MATTHEW 28:20)

26 April

And as we are – the world is. That is, if we are greedy,
envious, competitive, our society will be competitive,
envious, greedy, which brings misery and war. The State
is what we are. To bring about order and peace, we must
begin with ourselves and not with society, not with the
State, for the world is ourselves . . . If we would bring
about a sane and happy society we must begin with
ourselves and not with another, not outside of ourselves,
but with ourselves.

JIDDU KRISHNAMURTI

27 April

If the only prayer you ever say in your
entire life is thank you, it will be enough.

MEISTER ECKHART

28 April

I am not a product of my circumstances.
I am the product of my decisions.

STEPHEN COVEY

29 April

You should examine yourself daily.
If you find faults, you should
correct them. When you find
none, you should try even harder.

ANON

30 April

Make a habit of two things: to
help; or at least to do no harm.

HIPPOCRATES

Be Kind

We've heard a great deal in the media about kindness and how, as a nation, we need to try to be kinder. I wholeheartedly agree that many have lost sight of the fact that kindness is something innate; it's built in us. But the pressures of life, jealousy of others and our own inadequacies make us lose sight of this. Research has proved that showing kindness to others makes us happy, so why are so many ready to attack and be nasty rather than reach out and compliment or show the smallest act of caring? By doing these things we are, after all, only being true to our 'true' selves.

When we're kind to others – apparently, if the boffins are to be believed – we create neural pathways that enhance feelings of well-being via the natural flow of feel-good endorphins and mood-elevating neurotransmitters. Put in layman's terms: kindness makes you happier. It has also been proved that kindness can actually help you live longer. By being kind ourselves we encourage others to follow a similar path and, hopefully, we'll make the universe a better place.

I think it's also important to be kind to oneself. Personally, I have always been very tough on myself. I'm a bit of a perfectionist when it comes to work, always wanting to produce the best, and that can sometimes make me frustrated and negative. As I've got older I've learned to relax a lot more and take the rough with the smooth. And I've come to realise that love is more important than anything else. I'm a big fan of the expression 'It doesn't cost anything to be kind.' Kindness is the best free gift we can give. So be kind!

May is National Smile Month, and there is plenty to smile about. To start with, the month of May blesses us in the UK with two bank holidays, so an extra two whole days off. Surely that puts a smile on your face! The first of the month is May Day, celebrating the season of 'warmth and light'. It's also International Workers' Day or Labour Day, marking the campaign for workers' rights. I've been involved in many television shows that highlight the traditions of May Day and it's fair to say that they are all very colourful. Many involve the whole community coming together, which is always a great thing.

Think about the tradition of dancing around the maypole, for instance. The maypole is thought to go back to when pagans would cut down young trees, stick them in the ground and dance around them, holding competitions between rival villages. This dancing is thought to have evolved over the years into Morris dancing – and the young tree, to the maypole. According to the Morris dancing for all website (and yes, there is one!):

> The Morris dance is a form of English folk dance usually accompanied by music. It is based on rhythmic stepping and the execution of choreographed figures by a group of dancers, usually wearing bell pads on their shins. The dancers may also wield implements such as sticks and swords, and handkerchiefs may also be wielded by the dancers.

There are, by all accounts, written records of the Morris dance being enjoyed in England as far back as 1448, but only in refined surroundings. It wasn't until the sixteenth century that it was taken up by the lower classes too. I love the story of Shakespearean actor William Kempe, who Morris danced from London all the way to Norwich in 1600 and chronicled it in his *Nine Daies Wonder*. (I must suggest this a super idea for a Red Nose Day fundraiser, as long as I'm not the one doing the dancing!) The popularity of Morris dancing has come and gone over the centuries but, judging by what I've witnessed on my TV travels, it's still thriving in many parts of the country. I had a go about fifteen years ago and I'm hoping that the video will never surface. It's harder than it looks – I was sober too!

Around this wonderfully eccentric country there are quite a few weird and wonderful things you could be getting up to on May Day. For instance, you can put on a wooden or wicker frame covered in foliage and pretend you're Jack-in-the-Green. There's a huge Jack-in-the-Green festival in Hastings where the scary-looking character is released into the community. Or, how about heading to Padstow in Cornwall to see the Obby Oss, where they dress up as horses and try to catch a maiden (neigh! Surely not?!). My favourite, rather more elegant, tradition dates back at least 500 years and takes place in Oxford. It begins at 6.00 a.m. with the choristers of Magdalen College choir singing Hymnus Eucharisticus from the Great Tower. Hymnus Eucharisticus was composed in the seventeenth century by a Fellow of Magdalen College and has been sung every year since from the Great Tower on May Morning. The singing is always followed by bells ringing out over the city (and, in the past, by drunken students, who really should know better, jumping from Magdalen Bridge into the shallow River Cherwell).

Over on the Welsh–English border, for eleven days in May, many thousands of people come from all over the UK, Europe, America and the rest of the world to join a carnival celebration of ideas and stories at the Hay Festival. The programme of some 600 events takes place in the tented festival village during the spring bank holiday. Writers, politicians, poets, scientists, comedians, philosophers and musicians come together on the green-field site to talk, eat, think, drink and be merry. Richard Booth is recognised as the one responsible for transform-ing the town of Hay-on-Wye into a global attraction for secondhand book lovers after opening his first shop there in 1962. Nowadays, there are many more shops serving a population of nearly 2,000 people.

The Hay Festival is said to have been founded around a kitchen table back in 1987. Peter Florence discussed plans for a literary event with his parents Norman Flor-ence, a theatre manager and actor, and Rhoda Lewis, an actress. Just a year later, in May 1988, the Hay Festival of Literature and Arts was born. The number of festival-goers has increased dramatically over the years from the lower thousands in the early days to over 250,000 more recently. Such is its popularity that it has inspired similar cultural events in many countries, India and Mexico to name but two. Two US Presidents have visited the festi-val – Bill Clinton in 2001 and Jimmy Carter in 2008, with the former describing the place as 'the Woodstock of the mind'. My favourite bit of Hay trivia, though, is that singer-songwriter Ian Dury, of Blockheads fame, rewrote the lyrics to 'Hit Me With Your Rhythm Stick' at the festival, in what was to be one of his last concerts: 'From the gardens of Bombay, all the way to lovely Hay'. And I must confess to having a real love for the place too. I've visited many times and I even interviewed Melvyn Bragg there once, though I can't for the life of me remember why! I look forward to visiting for many years to come, God willing.

If Hay is the Woodstock of the mind, then the Eurovision Song Contest must be the playground for the bonkers! Although, just for the record, I've always adored the event, especially when my dear friend and 'radio dad' Terry Wogan used to present it (mainly for his wonderful asides). It was always a highlight of my May TV calendar.

So don't forget to smile this month, especially on the fourth, Star Wars Day: 'may the fourth be with you', and may you be a force for good and kindness, not just this month but always.

1 May

When I was five years old, my mother always told me that happiness was the key to life. When I went to school, they asked me what I wanted to be when I grew up. I wrote down 'happy'. They told me I didn't understand the assignment, and I told them they didn't understand life.

JOHN LENNON

2 May

This is my simple religion. There is no need for temples; no need for complicated philosophy. Our own brain, our own heart is our temple; the philosophy is kindness.

DALAI LAMA

3 May

There are those who give with joy, and that joy is their reward.

KHALIL GIBRAN

4 May

I always feel happy, you know why? Because I don't expect anything from anyone; expectations always hurt. Life is short, so love your life, be happy and keep smiling. Just live for yourself and before you speak, listen. Before you write, think. Before you spend, earn. Before you pray, forgive. Before you hurt, feel. Before you hate, love. Before you quit, try. Before you die, live.

ANON

5 May

True happiness is . . . to enjoy the present,
without anxious dependence upon the future.

SENECA

6 May

Always laugh when you can. It is cheap medicine.

LORD BYRON

7 May

Human greatness does not lie in wealth or power, but in character and goodness. People are just people, and all people have faults and shortcomings, but all of us are born with a basic goodness.

ANNE FRANK

8 May

Be kind, for everyone you
meet is fighting a hard battle.

ANON

9 May

Don't walk behind me; I may not lead.
Don't walk in front of me; I may not follow.
Just walk beside me and be my friend.

ALBERT CAMUS

10 May

The most valuable possession you can own is an open heart. The most powerful weapon you can be is an instrument of peace.

CARLOS SANTANA

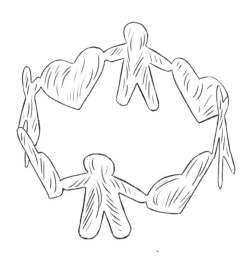

11 May

The best way to cheer yourself up is
to try to cheer somebody else up.

MARK TWAIN

12 May

Time spent laughing is time spent
with the gods.

JAPANESE PROVERB

13 May

You attract what you are, not what you want.

ANON

14 May

In the long run, the sharpest weapon of all is a kind and gentle spirit.

ANNE FRANK

15 May

I expect to pass through this world but once;
any good thing therefore that I can do, or any
kindness that I can show to my fellow creature,
let me do it now; let me not defer or neglect it,
for I shall not pass this way again.

STEPHEN GRELLET

16 May

One of the most spiritual things you can do is embrace your humanity. Connect with those around you today. Say, 'I love you', 'I'm sorry', 'I appreciate you', 'I'm proud of you' . . . whatever you're feeling. Send random texts, write a cute note, embrace your truth and share it . . . cause a smile today for someone else and give plenty of hugs.

STEVE MARABOLI

17 May

If you want others to be happy,
practise compassion.
If you want to be happy,
practise compassion.

DALAI LAMA

18 May

Mirth is like a flash of lightning that breaks through a gloom of clouds, and glitters for a moment: cheerfulness keeps up a kind of daylight in the mind.

JOSEPH ADDISON

19 May

The purpose of our lives is to be happy.

DALAI LAMA

20 May

There's a fine line between angry and grumpy.
Angry isn't nice, but grumpy is funny.

RICK WAKEMAN

21 May

What's the use of worrying?
It never was worthwhile,
So, pack up your troubles in your old kit bag,
And smile, smile, smile.

GEORGE ASAF

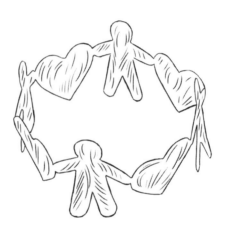

22 May

Better to be the one who smiled than the
one who didn't smile back.

ANON

23 May

There is nothing in the whole world so painful as feeling that one is not liked. It always seems to me that people who hate me must be suffering from some strange form of lunacy.

SEI SHŌNAGON

24 May

To succeed in life, you need
three things: a wishbone,
a backbone and a funny bone.

REBA MCENTIRE

25 May

Just as the soft rains fill the streams,
Pour into the rivers, and join together in the oceans,
So may the power of every moment of your goodness
Flow forth to awaken and heal all beings –
Those here now, those gone before, those yet to come.

By the power of every moment of your goodness,
May your heart's wishes be soon fulfilled
As completely shining as the bright full moon,
As magically as by a wish-fulfilling gem.

By the power of every moment of your goodness,
May all dangers be averted and all disease be gone.
May no obstacle come across your way.
May you enjoy fulfilment and long life.

For all in whose heart dwells respect,
Who follow the wisdom and compassion of the Way,
May your life prosper in the four blessings
Of old age, beauty, happiness and strength.

BUDHIST PRAYER AND HEALING CHANT

26 May

Happiness is the consequence of personal effort. You fight for it, strive for it, insist upon it, and sometimes even travel around the world looking for it. You have to participate relentlessly in the manifestations of your own blessings. And once you have achieved a state of happiness, you must never become lax about maintaining it, you must make a mighty effort to keep swimming upward into that happiness for ever, to stay afloat on top of it. If you don't, you will leak away your innate contentment. It's easy enough to pray when you're in distress but continuing to pray even when your crisis has passed is like a sealing process, helping your soul hold tight to its good attainments.

ELIZABETH GILBERT

27 May

Start every day off with a smile
and get it over with.

W.C. FIELDS

28 May

Some folks rail against other folks,
because other folks have what some
folks would be glad of.

HENRY FIELDING

29 May

The unthankful heart discovers no mercies;
but the thankful heart will find, in every
hour, some heavenly blessings.

HENRY WARD BEECHER

30 May

It is not how much we have, but how much
we enjoy, that makes happiness.

CHARLES SPURGEON

31 May

If there were no coincidence,
it would be the greatest
coincidence of all.

G.K. CHESTERTON

Summer Sunshine

Sun, songs and serious serves! That's what June means to me. It's a month filled with events of global importance which all happen here in the UK. And guess what? The songs and serious serves only reach their zenith with the sun shining down on them. Enough of the cryptic clues, I'm talking about the two events that are music at Glastonbury and tennis at Wimbledon. Let's start with the sun, shall we?

In the northern hemisphere the day of the summer solstice is the longest day of the year and occurs each year between 20 and 22 June. Solstice – Litha for pagans and Alban Hefin ('light of summer' or 'light of the shore') for modern druids – means a stopping or standing still of the sun. And here comes the science bit: it occurs when the earth's geographical pole on either the northern or southern hemisphere becomes most inclined towards the sun. When the summer solstice takes place in the northern hemisphere, the sun will reach its highest possible point. As a result, the day on which the summer solstice falls will have the longest period of daylight of the year – makes sense, right? Around the time of the summer solstice, areas of Norway, Finland, Greenland, Russia, Alaska in the United States and parts of Canada experience 'midnight sun'. In Svalbard in Norway, which is the most northerly inhabited region of Europe, there is no sunset for about four months. I loved this fact as a child because it would mean I could be outdoors playing football literally all day and night! 'Hurra!' as they'd say in Norway (it means hooray and, yes, I had to look it up).

Throughout history the summer solstice or midsummer has been a very special date in the diary for many diverse cultures around the world, particularly pagans. In England, thousands of pagans and non-pagans alike travel to ancient religious sites such as Stonehenge and Avebury. Revellers typically gather at Stonehenge, the ancient stone circle in Wiltshire, where the Heel Stone and Slaughter Stone, set outside the main circle, align with the rising sun. I've only ever seen this on TV but it looks incredible. Unless, of course, it's raining. But even then the spirits of those gathered there aren't dampened, with many bedecked in full costume.

Stonehenge is the world's most famous stone circle. It's believed to have been an important religious site as far back as 4,000 years ago and more than a million people visit it each year. It's a fantastical monument to all that is mysterious and overwhelming about our past (even if you only encounter it while whizzing along the A303). For well over a century, people have congregated there to celebrate the summer solstice and these days it can draw crowds of more than 30,000 people of all ages and backgrounds. The event is considered to represent empowerment, healing and new life. It's a time of great reflection and hope, an opportunity to take stock of the past and look to a positive future.

I'm told that, traditionally, people would stay up all night on midsummer's eve to welcome the sunrise. Bonfires would be lit on tops of hills, by holy wells and at sacred places, to praise the fullness of the sun. At Litha the bonfire represents a reflection of the sun at the peak of its power. The oak tree was and still is seen as a very important symbol, as are aromatic herbs, which are scattered into the fire. People danced and made merry, a tradition that carries on to this day. The Celtic name for oak is 'duir' which means 'doorway'. I like the idea that the summer solstice signifies that we are traversing the threshold of nature and moving into the second, fading, part of the year, where the sun will gradually lose its power. From now on days grow shorter and nights longer; we are drawn back into the dark to complete, as the pagans call it, the Wheel of the Year. I find such symbolism really powerful.

Just over fifty miles to the west of Stonehenge lies Glastonbury, another place of pilgrimage, today mostly for music lovers, as it's home to the world's biggest performing arts festival. Oh, how the organisers must pray for sun every year – we've all witnessed the scenes of muddy hell when it rains! But come rain or shine, hundreds of thousands of festivalgoers descend upon Worthy Farm in Somerset to enjoy music, comedy, live acts and create some memories to savour. And yours truly has been lucky enough to perform there. Now, before you run off to type in 'Has Aled Jones performed on the pyramid stage?' on Google, let me pre-empt you to say, no, I haven't! I actually got to perform on a classical night in the Glastonbury Extravaganza, which is a three-day event that the festival organisers hold to say thanks to locals for putting up with the partying mayhem that goes hand in hand with the main affair. But as far as I'm concerned, I've played Glastonbury! I even got to share the stage briefly with the colourful and endearing character that is Michael Eavis, the co-creator of Glastonbury.

My Glastonbury experience pales into insignificance, however, compared to when I played tennis on the hallowed grass courts of Wimbledon. It's true, honestly! I can assure you I'm not having a Walter Mitty moment, indulging in fantastic daydreams of personal triumphs. Let me explain. Those of a certain age will remember that, when it started to rain at Wimbledon during the 1980s and 1990s, along would come a smartly dressed man talking into a walkie-talkie at the far end of Centre Court, anxiously glancing upwards at the sky in search of rain clouds. You'd pray that he didn't suspend play, but he always did. That man was Alan Mills, the then Wimbledon referee. He was a fan of my boy chorister music and invited me to join him for a match at Wimbledon. I was in seventh heaven!

What many people don't know is that I've always been a huge tennis fan, and in the past a voracious player. In fact, when my voice broke, tennis took over my life for a bit and I played up to six hours a day. So I took up Alan's invitation eagerly and along I went with every intention of beating a man four or five times my age. I fancied myself as the Welsh Boris Becker. What I hadn't realised was that the Wimbledon referee, older than my dad, was also an accomplished tennis player who had got into the last sixteen of the Wimbledon tournament himself . . . twice. He was also the first man in the history of the Davis Cup to win a match with the score line 6–0, 6–0, 6–0. We only played one set, and the score line? You've guessed it: 6–0 in his favour! I was demolished, but loved every moment of it. It was a pleasure to share the court with him and I was so thankful to see the other side of Wimbledon (Alan was also very gracious in inviting me to the tournament every year while he was referee). When we shook hands at the net and walked back to the changing room together, Alan turned to me and said, 'Stick to the singing, kid!' So I did! I still play for fun though, and enjoy nothing more than toasting summer with a Pimm's and lemonade at the world's greatest tennis tournament.

1 June

Let us give thanks for our shadows
for they are there in the first place
because of the presence of light.

KAMAND KOJOURI

2 June

Deep peace of the running wave to you.
Deep peace of the flowing air to you.
Deep peace of the quiet earth to you.
Deep peace of the shining stars to you.
Deep peace of the gentle night to you.
Moon and stars pour their healing light on you.
Deep peace of Christ the light of the world to you.
Deep peace of Christ to you.

GAELIC BLESSING

3 June

In order for the light to shine so brightly,
the darkness must be present.

FRANCIS BACON

4 June

May togetherness of this earth continue
to guide us, and may the divine bring peace
and understanding to protect the world.

NIGERIAN PRAYER

5 June

We must be willing to let go of the life we planned so as to have the life that is waiting for us.

JOSEPH CAMPBELL

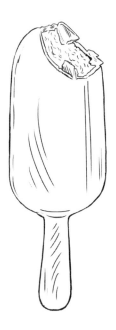

6 June

May flowers always line your path and sunshine light
   your day.
May songbirds serenade you every step along the way.
May a rainbow run beside you in a sky that's always blue.
And may happiness fill your heart each day your whole
   life through.

IRISH BLESSING

7 June

Take risks. If you win, you will be happy. If you lose,
you will be wise.

ANON

8 June

So the darkness shall be the light,
and the stillness the dancing.

T.S. ELIOT

9 June

Humankind has not woven the web of life.
We are but one thread within it.
Whatever we do to the web, we do to ourselves.
All things are bound together. All things connect.

CHIEF SEATTLE

10 June

Keep your face always toward the sunshine –
and shadows will fall behind you.

WALT WHITMAN

11 June

Life is not about waiting for the storm to pass
but learning to dance in the rain.

VIVIAN GREENE

12 June

Free yourself from your past mistakes, by forgiving yourself for what you have done or went through. Every day is another chance to start over.

ANON

13 June

Your mind is a powerful thing. When you fill it with positive thoughts, your life will start to change.

ANON

14 June

Two roads diverged in a wood, and I –
I took the one less travelled by,
And that has made all the difference.

ROBERT FROST

15 June

Sometimes we stare so long at a door that is
closing that we see too late the one that is open.

ALEXANDER GRAHAM BELL

16 June

I will love the light for it shows me the way,
yet I will endure the darkness because it shows
me the stars.

OG MANDINO

17 June

It is during our darkest moments
that we must focus to see the light.

ANON

18 June

In the end, only three things matter:
how much you loved, how gently you
lived, and how gracefully you let go of
things not meant for you.

ANON

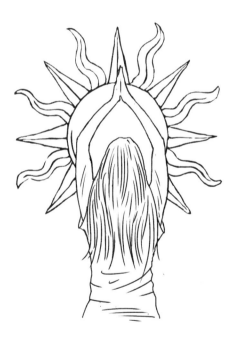

19 June

If you cannot find peace within yourself,
you will never find it anywhere else.

MARVIN GAYE

20 June

There is a crack in everything.
That's how the light gets in.

LEONARD COHEN

21 June

Words are like leaves; and where they most abound,
Much fruit of sense beneath is rarely found.

ALEXANDER POPE

22 June

I am prepared for the worst, but hope for the best.

BENJAMIN DISRAELI

23 June

Your time is coming. It's about to happen for
you. So many breakthroughs. So many blessings.
Keep believing and watch your life change.

ANON

24 June

Reflect upon your present blessings – of which every man has many – not on your past misfortunes, of which all men have some.

CHARLES DICKENS

25 June

Experience is the name everyone gives to
their mistakes.

OSCAR WILDE

26 June

Only in the darkness can you see the stars.

MARTIN LUTHER KING, JR

27 June

Looking behind, I am filled with gratitude.
Looking forward, I am filled with vision.
Looking upwards, I am filled with strength.
Looking within, I discover peace.

May the stars carry your sadness away.
May the flowers fill your heart with beauty.
May hope forever wipe away your tears.
And, above all, may silence make you strong.

QUEIO APACHE PRAYER

28 June

And above all, watch with glittering eyes the
whole world around you because the greatest secrets
are always hidden in the most unlikely places.
Those who don't believe in magic will never find it.

ROALD DAHL

29 June

Lord, make me an instrument of thy peace.
Where there is hatred, let me sow love.

FRANCIS OF ASSISI

30 June

Between us and excellence, the gods have placed the sweat of our brows.

HESIOD

Childhood Memories

'So are you sitting comfortably, class? This is your last history lesson of the academic year.' Little Aled Jones would be sitting very comfortably indeed, brimming with excitement and nervous energy, no less. Just an hour to go before life would change in a very pleasant way! 'Turn to page 7 and we're looking at the month of July.'

July is named after Julius Caesar by a decision of the Roman Senate in 44 BC, July being the month of his birth. Before that, it had been known as Quintilis, Latin for 'fifth', as it was the fifth month in the earliest calendar attributed to Romulus. Until the eighteenth century, the word's English pronunciation focused heavily on the first syllable, making it rhyme with words like 'truly' or 'duly'.

Come on, admit it, who else at this point is thinking of Ali G and Shaggy's hit 'Me Julie'? (My mind wandered a lot in class!)

In the sporting world back in 1877, the inaugural Wimbledon Tennis Championships began in this month. In the music world a teenage John Lennon and Paul McCartney met for the first time in July 1957, three years before forming the Beatles. Just two years earlier, Disneyland had opened in California. And not so much Dumbo, but who can forget that jumbo off-script incident on BBC television's *Blue Peter*, back in July 1969, when Lulu the elephant became one of the first 'pooper bloopers'. But a defining moment of my adolescent years also happened in July. In 1979 the Walkman was introduced to the world. It became my lifeline on endless train journeys from North Wales to London, every weekend when I was singing as a boy soprano. I would escape into my own musical world of Spandau Ballet, Curiosity Killed the Cat, Deacon Blue and the soundtrack to the musical *Les Misérables*, while every other person in the carriage stared at me, gossipping and giggling (my dad made me travel standard class to 'keep it real' – not such a welcome simple pleasure, I have to confess!).

July is also known for being the midway point of the year. However, just for the record, that actually falls on the third day of the month, rather than the first. It's also supposedly the warmest month in the UK, and a federal holiday is held on 4 July in the United States of America, commemorating the Declaration of Independence. July's birthstone, the ruby, is said to symbolise contentment. And that's precisely how I felt when that last school bell rang at 3.30 p.m. on the Friday before the summer holidays – independent, free and so content! I wasn't the only happy one – my fellow pupils were equally elated, as was my mother who was a primary school teacher; I witnessed the term's pressure visibly dropping off her shoulders on the car journey home on break-up Friday.

Isn't it funny how times change? Nowadays, within hours of the school holidays hitting, many families are already at the airport jetting off to ski or sunbathe, deserting Britain for somewhere more glamorous. I'm not complaining one bit, and positively welcome the exodus, because it means I can park easily where I live and there are no queues at the supermarket! But as a child I didn't crave the buzzing Balearics or the sun, sea and sand of the Algarve. Equally, I didn't need an action-packed après-ski in Chamonix. I always loved the summer holidays though. Back in the 1970s and 1980s the world seemed to be a much smaller place. (Before you comment, I realise that the world back then was the same size as it is now – I did at least pay attention in geography classes.) When I was growing up though, my world revolved around my little village, and that extended no further than a two-mile radius. This was my playground. And do you know what? I needed nothing more to keep me entertained for the entire six-week holiday.

Even as I write this, there's a nostalgic smile on my face as the memories come flooding back of a much more innocent, gentler and, dare I say it, safer time. Everything was just simpler. People would ask, 'What plans do you have for the summer holidays?' and my parents or I would answer, 'Nothing'. If I said that now, in front of my children, I think they may well never speak to me again (unless they had a fully charged iPad!). Back then, however, every moment of my summer break would be filled with adventures that were so liberating and character-forming. It wasn't that my parents neglected me, far from it – I was cared for just perfectly. But they trusted me and I thrived on the autonomy. I'd stuff a wrapped-up jam sandwich on white bread into my shorts pocket and, with a shout of 'See you later – I'll be back when it's dark!' I'd be out of the door. No other details were offered and none was asked for. Not a watch or a mobile phone in sight. And who knew what the day would bring? The simple pleasures of bike rides and tree climbing. Chasing girls and big heavy footballs. Grass stains on the knees from sliding tackles. Trousers ripped from jumping endless barbed-wire fences (sometimes illegally, sorry Mr Farmer!). Fishing and swimming, hide-and-seek and its variant Block 123 (also known as Forty Forty and 123 Home). I also remember secretly listening to a Sex

Pistols' single on my best friend's older brother's record player. We thought we were so grown up and edgy!

So why not approach this summer in a different, less pressured way? And this is coming from someone who, many times in the past, has spent hours browsing on the Internet in the hope of finding that life-changing bargain holiday in the sun. But the height of summer doesn't have to be about the perfectly chilled beer next to the perfect pool, in the perfect hotel or villa. Take a tip from young Aled and take a step back, remembering those Julys of yesteryear. Go on a physical trip down memory lane and think back to those 'perfect' simple pleasures that were free and easy. I wish I'd savoured them more at the time. It's never too late to retreat, to approach things more slowly and live in the moment, take a deep breath in the fresh air and enjoy the warm summer breeze. I plan to embrace these simple pleasures more in the future.

1 July

Life is not about receiving at all times; it is a combination of being thankful for what you have as blessings and sharing those blessings with others who need a little fraction of what you have.

CATHERINE PULSIFER

2 July

You don't learn to walk by
following rules. You learn by doing,
and by falling over.

RICHARD BRANSON

3 July

My belief is that we were put into this world of wonders and beauty with a special ability to appreciate them, in some cases to have the fun of taking a hand in developing them, and also in being able to help other people instead of overreaching them and, through it all, to enjoy life – that is, to be happy.

ROBERT BADEN-POWELL

4 July

In character, in manner, in style, in all things, the supreme excellence is simplicity.

HENRY WADSWORTH LONGFELLOW

5 July

The secret of genius is to carry the spirit of the child into old age, which means never losing your enthusiasm.

ALDOUS HUXLEY

6 July

Blessed is he who expects nothing, for he shall never be disappointed.

ALEXANDER POPE

7 July

There's only one thing more precious than our time and that's what we spend it on.

LEO CHRISTOPHER

8 July

Cherish what you have because not all people are blessed with the things that you are enjoying.

FAITH STARR

9 July

A little toil and a little rest,
And a little more earned than spent,
Is sure to bring to an honest breast
A blessing of glad content.

NIXON WATERMAN

10 July

May the God of the sun, gently rising
Bring the hope of a day just begun.
May the God of the oceans all around us
Bring you the peace of the Holy One.

May the God of the desert, heart of our land
Bring the stillness and silence of the wise.
May the God of the rivers, flowing freely.
Bring new hope, soothing calm, and new life.

May the God of blue skies above us
Lift your heart and bring you joy.
May the God of the rains from the heavens
Nurture you and soothe your soul.

May the God of the sun, gently setting
Bring you peace and rest your weary heart.
May the God of the stars of our Southern Cross
Shine down on you wherever you are.
Shine down on you wherever you are.

ANDREW CHINN

11 July

No one is free, even the birds are chained to the sky.

BOB DYLAN

12 July

Find much to be grateful for in every day.
Doing so will not only enrich your life, it will bless
those around you in ways you may never know.

RICHELLE E. GOODRICH

13 July

There is one thing which gives
radiance to everything. It is the idea
of something around the corner.

G.K. CHESTERTON

14 July

Live your life. Take chances. Be crazy. Don't wait. Because right now is the oldest you've ever been and the youngest you'll ever be again.

SUZANNE COLLINS

15 July

Start by doing what's necessary; then do what's possible; and suddenly you are doing the impossible.

FRANCIS OF ASSISI

16 July

It's better to be a lion for a day than a sheep all your life.

ELIZABETH KENNY

17 July

Do not go where the path may lead, go instead where there is no path and leave a trail.

RALPH WALDO EMERSON

18 July

You only live once, but if you
do it right, once is enough.

MAE WEST

19 July

Life is like a camera. Just focus on what's
important, capture the good times,
develop from the negatives, and if things
don't work out, just take another shot.

ANON

20 July

God gave us the gift of life; it is up to us to give ourselves the gift of living well.

VOLTAIRE

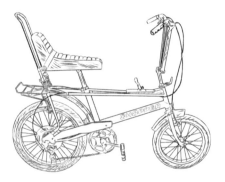

21 July

They laugh at me because I'm different;
I laugh at them because they are all the same.

KURT COBAIN

22 July

No matter what challenges or setbacks and disappointments you may encounter along the way, you will find true success and happiness if you have only one goal. There really is only one. And that is this: to fulfil the highest, most truthful expression of yourself as a human being. You want to max out your humanity by using your energy to lift yourself up, your family and the people around you.

OPRAH WINFREY

23 July

Be where you are; otherwise you will miss your life.

ANON

24 July

If you want to feel rich, just count the things you have that money can't buy.

ANON

25 July

Mix a little foolishness with
your prudence: it's good to be
silly at the right moment.

HORACE

26 July

You have to learn the rules of the game. And then you have to play better than anyone else.

ANON

27 July

You cannot swim for new horizons until you have courage to lose sight of the shore.

WILLIAM FAULKNER

28 July

Few will have the greatness to bend history itself, but each of us can work to change a small portion of events . . . it is from numberless acts of courage and belief that human history is shaped.

ROBERT F. KENNEDY

29 July

If you realised how powerful your thoughts are, you would never think a negative thought.

PEACE PILGRIM

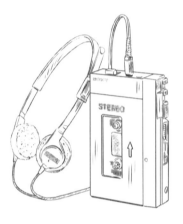

30 July

Today you are you!
That is truer than true!
There is no one alive
Who is you-er than you!

DR SEUSS

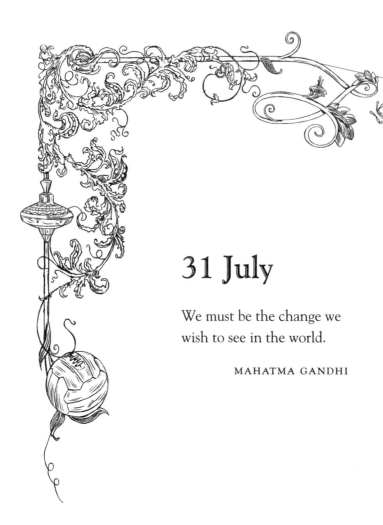

31 July

We must be the change we
wish to see in the world.

MAHATMA GANDHI

The Arts

The arts are often seen as 'soft' subjects at school, tending to be overlooked in favour of the more 'useful' subjects like maths or science. I have always believed this is grossly unfair: music and the creative arts are the joy of civilisation. I've noticed from being a parent to two teenagers that there is undoubtedly increasing pressure on young people and schools to achieve outstanding exam results in core subjects. But the arts in education should not be seen as a luxury and we must fight to keep the arts at the heart of our society.

It was the nineteenth-century English critic John Ruskin who said, 'Life without industry is guilt, and industry without art is brutality.' The benefits of the arts in education are well documented. Certainly, music makes you a better learner, the skills that come with learning an instrument and the discipline of practising being transferable to any other subject. Music and the arts can also give confidence to those who lack it and can help one relax in a very fast-moving and pressured world. Playing an instrument, drawing or painting, performing a play, or singing in a choir is the time when young people especially are at their happiest and such time can deeply enrich the rest of their lives. Being a member of an orchestra, choir or drama production brings people of all ages together and encourages teamwork and support. It's also a super-social experience, which I know only too well, and it seems many adults have cottoned on to the benefits of interacting creatively too, with the explosion of new choirs popping up everywhere. It's not just about making that perfect sound, it's about making any sound with like-minded people and often going for a drink afterwards. It's about making relationships and enjoying a sense of fellowship. It's the perfect way to switch off from the stresses and strains of everyday life. So, we overlook the value of music and the arts in education at our peril.

I was very lucky in attending a primary and comprehensive school where music played a vital role; it wasn't unusual for the guitar to be brought out by the maths or geography teacher! As a super enthusiastic five-year-old, performing in front of mum and dad in my first nativity, I got my bug for acting by playing a curtain-wearing Joseph in the school production of *Joseph and the Amazing Technicolour Dreamcoat*, a role I was later fortunate enough to reprise in Andrew Lloyd Webber's West End production (the quality of Joseph's coat was significantly more professional second time round). That vital performance seed was sown back in Llandegfan Primary School and I'm so thankful to the staff there for inspiring us creatively and allowing us to embrace the arts.

It's interesting to note that, in times of need, such as we have experienced lately with the dreadful coronavirus pandemic, the arts are the very subjects people turn to first and foremost for comfort and inspiration. Music and the arts not only make us feel good, they also have the ability to transport us away from our personal cares and take us somewhere else. Nowhere is this more evident than in Edinburgh during the month of August. Its Fringe Festival is the single biggest celebration of arts and culture on the planet. Every August, for three weeks, the city welcomes an explosion of creative energy from around the globe. Performers take to stages across the city to present shows for every taste. From big household names in the world of entertainment to unknown artists looking to build their careers. You can experience theatre, comedy, dance, circus, cabaret, children's shows, music, musicals, opera, spoken word, exhibitions and tons of other events.

I'll never forget the first time I went up to the Fringe Festival. I was hosting a special edition of *Songs of Praise* from the event and could sense the palpable air of adrenaline and positive energy the minute I got off the train. As I was there to film a TV show, I got to see the best of the event by interviewing some of the big-named stars as well as performers on the first rung of the ladder of success, and I got to mingle with the crowd. My TV crew realised straightaway that we were also centre of attention when the camera was rolling: it was evident that everyone thought that they should be presenting *Songs of Praise*, not just me. I don't think I managed to do one piece to camera (that's speaking a link to camera in TV talk) without someone with a larger-than-life personality jumping in front of me!

A lot of our filming was done on the Royal Mile, arguably the most famous thoroughfare in Scotland's capital city and sometimes known as Edinburgh's High Street. It's at the heart of Edinburgh's Old Town, with Edinburgh Castle at its head and the Palace of Holyroodhouse at its foot. Its name comes from its tradition as a processional route for kings and queens for the last 500 years. It first gained its nickname in 1901, thanks to W.M. Gilbert's book, *Edinburgh in the Nineteenth Century*. And, just for the record, the Royal Mile is almost exactly one mile (just over 1.6 kilometres) long; guidebooks tell you it takes roughly twenty-five minutes to walk it end to end.

But, let me tell you, that is decidedly not the case during the Fringe Festival when you have camera, sound and director with you! We spent the best part of a day walking from one end to the other in the blistering heat and it's an experience I'll never forget! The sights, the sounds and the smells were intoxicating. We were confronted by street buskers, eager Fringe performers pushing their show flyers into our hands, and food and accents from all over the world. It was literally a melting pot of creativity and I relished every second of it. I've been back to the Festival many times since and would one day love to perform there myself.

August can be a busy time for a singer and performer, although there are now fewer festivals and open-air concerts than there used to be. I simply adore an outside concert and the thrill of the unexpected. Will it rain? Will the orchestra's sheet music be blown off their music stands? (They actually use clothes pegs to keep the music in place!) Will the crowd get drunk during the proms bit? (I was once confronted by an inebriated old lady gyrating and blowing kisses at me during 'Land of Hope and Glory'. To this day I don't know how I managed to continue to sing. My fellow performer, who shall remain nameless, was in hysterics.) But what I love about these events is that they bring the whole community together. It could be 5,000 people in a field in the pouring rain with a hundred-piece orchestra and performers on stage, and yet we are all there for one reason, and that is to feel good. We are there to experience a magic that we can't put into words. And for me that's the power of the arts. They enhance and improve everyone's lives.

1 August

I never had a policy; I have
just tried to do my very best
each and every day.

ABRAHAM LINCOLN

2 August

Follow your passion, be prepared to work hard and sacrifice, and, above all, don't let anyone limit your dreams.

DONOVAN BAILEY

3 August

The biggest adventure you can take is to
live the life of your dreams.

OPRAH WINFREY

4 August

Talent hits a target no one else can hit;
genius hits a target no one else can see.

ARTHUR SCHOPENHAUER

5 August

Ability is what you're capable of doing.
Motivation determines what you do.
Attitude determines how well you do it.

LOU HOLTZ

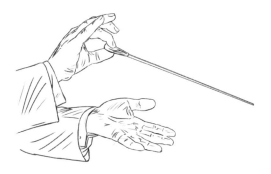

6 August

Just don't give up trying to do what you
really want to do. Where there is love and
inspiration, I don't think you can go wrong.

ELLA FITZGERALD

7 August

A dream doesn't become reality
through magic; it takes sweat,
determination and hard work.

COLIN POWELL

8 August

You are never too old to set another goal or to dream a new dream.

C.S. LEWIS

9 August

I'm playing all the right notes, but not
necessarily in the right order.

ERIC MORECAMBE

10 August

Believe in yourself. You are braver than you think, more talented than you know, and capable of more than you imagine.

ROY T. BENNETT

11 August

Stay true to yourself, yet always be open to learn. Work hard, and never give up on your dreams, even when nobody else believes they can come true but you. These are not clichés but real tools you need no matter what you do in life to stay focused on your path.

PHILLIP SWEET

12 August

Believe you can and you're halfway there.

THEODORE ROOSEVELT

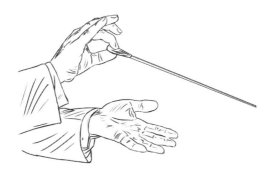

13 August

There is no great genius without some touch of madness.

ARISTOTLE

14 August

Success is no accident. It is hard work, perseverance, learning, studying, sacrifice and most of all, love of what you are doing or learning to do.

PELÉ

15 August

When I wake up every morning . . . I find something creative to do with my life.

MILES DAVIS

16 August

The more you lose yourself in
something bigger than yourself,
the more energy you will have.

NORMAN VINCENT PEALE

17 August

The glory is being happy. The glory is not winning here or winning there. The glory is enjoying practising, enjoying every day, enjoying to work hard, trying to be a better player than before.

RAFAEL NADAL

18 August

Shoot for the moon and if you miss you will still be among the stars.

LES BROWN

19 August

Big shots are only little shots who keep shooting.

CHRISTOPHER MORLEY

20 August

All life is an experiment. The more experiments you make the better.

RALPH WALDO EMERSON

21 August

Once we believe in ourselves, we can risk
curiosity, wonder, spontaneous delight, or any
experience that reveals the human spirit.

E.E. CUMMINGS

22 August

Creativity is contagious. Pass it on.

ALBERT EINSTEIN

23 August

It is never too late to be what
you might have been.

GEORGE ELIOT

24 August

Only those who will risk going too far can possibly find out how far one can go.

T.S. ELIOT

25 August

Always be a first-rate version of yourself and
not a second-rate version of someone else.

JUDY GARLAND

26 August

There is no better than adversity. Every defeat, every heartbreak, every loss, contains its own seed, its own lesson on how to improve your performance the next time.

MALCOLM X

27 August

Positive thinking will let you do everything better than negative thinking will.

ZIG ZIGLAR

28 August

There are no short cuts to any place worth going.

BEVERLY SILLS

29 August

The same stream of life that runs through
my veins night and day runs through the
world and dances in rhythmic measures.
It is the same life that shoots in joy
through the dust of the earth into
numberless blades of grass and breaks into
tumultuous waves of leaves and flowers.

RABINDRANATH TAGORE

30 August

You only pass through this life once,
you don't come back for an encore.

ELVIS PRESLEY

31 August

The best revenge is to live
on and prove yourself.

EDDIE VEDDER

Back to School

When I was a schoolboy, September meant one thing to me and that was that life was going back to normal. It was the month that served up a great big, smack-in-the-chops reality check after the glorious six weeks of summer holidays. The huge realisation of 'back to school' would hit me when my mother would take me into Bangor, our closest city and where I was a chorister at the cathedral, on the hunt for a new pencil case and school bag. And, depending on growth, maybe even a new pair of trousers and shoes. Usually the promise of some new clobber would make me happy. But this shop with mum meant no more carefree days running wild around my village with my friends; it meant the imminent return of homework, the dreaded school uniform and routine. Don't get me wrong, I had a super group of friends at school, and we had a lot of fun. I just wasn't too keen on the bits in between the fun – the double geography and the utter hell of chemistry or maths (I've always been more of an arts boy!).

The month of September could have been much longer. Up until 1752, the calendar we used in the UK was the Julian calendar. It was based on the solar year which is the time it takes for the earth to rotate around the sun. The Julian calendar was 365 *and a quarter* days long, and not the most accurate – over time, it became out of sync with the seasons. So in 1752 Britain dumped the Julian calendar in favour of the Gregorian calendar and, in doing so, lost eleven days when the third day of September instantly became the fourteenth. There were, by some accounts, huge protests in the streets because people thought their lives would be shortened! (Some experts now dispute this actually happened, but I like the story.)

September in Old English was called 'Haervest Monath', meaning 'harvest month', a time to gather up the rest of the harvest and prepare for the winter. And I certainly remember Harvest Festivals in school and church, where we'd sing, pray and decorate the spaces with fruit and food – school assembly would always be awash with the tin cans no one wanted! Also called 'harvest home', Harvest Festival was traditionally held on or near the Sunday of the Harvest Moon – the full moon that occurs closest to the autumn equinox, around 22–24 September. It was a time of thanksgiving that involved the whole community, young and old, with lavish meals, plenty of drink, song, dance and making merry. The Harvest Moon occurs in September most years, but around every three years, it appears in October. The tradition of celebrating Harvest Festival in churches began in 1843, when Reverend Robert Hawker invited parishioners from his church in the Cornish parish of Morwenstow to his home for a special thanksgiving service.

Another event that signalled dwindling summer days when I was growing up was the Last Night of the Proms, which marks the end of the season of summer concerts broadcast all over the world from the Royal Albert Hall in London. One of my earliest memories is of hearing my father heartily singing along with the Promenaders from the comfort of his couch. But little did I know back then that the Royal Albert Hall would become such a huge part of my life. I made my debut there as a twelve-year-old boy soprano and have even played tennis there against American Zina Garrison, who was ranked number four in the world at the time. She challenged me to a game during her warm-up for the Whiteman Cup, a US-versus-UK women's tournament that I happened to be presenting when I was seventeen. She thrashed me, but we had lots of fun trying to knock our tennis balls into the acoustic diffusers known as 'mushrooms' hanging from the ceiling. (I was told by management that, when they took them down many years later to clean, they found two tennis balls and a pair of false teeth in one of them. The teeth were nothing to do with Zena or me but I apologise if my tennis ball had any detrimental effects on the sound quality!) What an honour it was to be included in Sir Peter Blake's mural of performers who have graced the stage there the most, sandwiched between conductors Claudio Abbado and Sir Charles Mackerras no less!

For many years the Last Night of the Proms came to mean something completely different for me though. It signified that I would be in a packed-out Royal Albert Hall the following day in order to present and sing in the *Songs of Praise Big Sing*. I hosted it for over fifteen years and loved the event so much; nothing compares to hearing a hymn like 'How Great Thou Art' being sung by over 5,000 people. It was also very special being there the morning after the night before. The electricity of the Last Night was still very much in the air.

Another September *Songs of Praise* memory takes me to my beloved Blackpool where I met my wife while playing Joseph in the musical which was camped there for the whole summer season. Now, I've never been asked to turn on the famous Blackpool Illuminations, but I am one of a very select bunch who have switched them off! The first set of Illuminations was introduced in 1879 when the council devoted the sum of £5,000 to experiment with the concept of electric street lighting, starting with eight arc lamps on sixty-feet poles in Talbot Square. There are now six miles of traditional festoons and tableaux along the Promenade and illuminated tram cars aplenty. It's an amazing spectacle and well worth the trip. I was presenting a *Songs of Praise* summer special from Blackpool and had a unique dispensation to switch the whole of the Prom lights off during one of my links to camera. The timing had to be absolutely precise and, by some fluke, I managed to deliver the lines and push the button at exactly the right moment. The entire stretch of the Promenade went pitch black. Oh, the power at my fingertips! (This honestly did happen, but you'll have to take my word for it because, owing to time issues, it didn't make the final programme. The producer still owes me a drink for taking it out of the cut!)

If, like me, you find it a bit difficult to get back to normal after the summer holidays, treat yourself to a trip to Cumbria on the third Saturday in September and make sure you go to the Egremont Crab Fair. It was established back in 1267, which makes it one of the oldest fairs in the world. Its combination of traditional events with modern attractions in ever creative ways draws visitors from all around the globe. It's also home to the World Gurning Championships where contestants contort their features and the prize goes to the one who makes the most appalling or shocking face. I could well have been a contender for the top prize when I was a youngster as I stepped off the bus on the first day back at school.

1 September

By working faithfully eight hours a
day, you may eventually get to be
a boss and work twelve hours a day.

ROBERT FROST

2 September

Never let the future disturb you.
You will meet it, if you have to, with
the same weapons of reason which
today arm you against the present.

MARCUS AURELIUS

3 September

The scariest moment is always just
before you start.

STEPHEN KING

4 September

When you come to the end of your
rope, tie a knot and hang on.

FRANKLIN D. ROOSEVELT

5 September

Anyone who stops learning is old, whether at twenty or eighty. Anyone who keeps learning stays young. The greatest thing in life is to keep your mind young.

HENRY FORD

6 September

The only thing that I have done that is not mitigated by luck, diminished by good fortune, is that I persisted, and other people gave up.

HARRISON FORD

7 September

The harder I work, the luckier I get.

GARY PLAYER

8 September

Nothing in life is to be feared,
it is only to be understood.
Now is the time to understand
more so that we may fear less.

MARIE CURIE

9 September

This is a friendly reminder that you
will only get a limited time on this earth.
Today is a good day to do something great.

ANON

10 September

We're born alone, we live alone, we die alone. Only through our love and friendship can we create the illusion for the moment that we're not alone.

ORSON WELLES

11 September

Stay positive. Sometimes you don't even realise you're blocking your own blessings by thinking negatively and holding on to the past. Learn to let go.

GERMANY KENT

12 September

Plan your work for today and every day,
then work your plan.

MARGARET THATCHER

13 September

Our greatest glory is not in never falling,
but in rising every time we fall.

CONFUCIUS

14 September

The hardest arithmetic to master is that which
enables us to count our blessings.

ERIC HOFFER

15 September

Those born to wealth, and who have the means
of gratifying every wish, know not what is the real
happiness of life, just as those who have been tossed
on the stormy waters of the ocean on a few frail
planks can alone realise the blessings of fair weather.

ALEXANDRE DUMAS

16 September

Some people come in your life as blessings.
Some come in your life as lessons.

MOTHER TERESA

17 September

Don't cry because it's over.
Smile because it happened.

DR SEUSS

18 September

You gain strength, courage, and confidence by every experience in which you really stop to look fear in the face . . . The danger lies in refusing to face the fear, in not daring to come to grips with it . . . You must make yourself succeed every time. You must do the thing you think you cannot do.

ELEANOR ROOSEVELT

19 September

Promise me you'll always remember:
You're braver than you believe, and stronger
than you seem, and smarter than you think.

A.A. MILNE

20 September

If you fell down yesterday, stand up today.

H.G. WELLS

21 September

If you don't like something, change it; if you can't change it, change the way you think about it.

MARY ENGELBREIT

22 September

Hope is important because it can make the present moment less difficult to bear. If we believe that tomorrow will be better, we can bear a hardship today.

THICH NHAT HANH

23 September

I learned that courage was not the absence of fear, but the triumph over it. The brave man is not he who does not feel afraid, but he who conquers that fear.

NELSON MANDELA

24 September

Fear doesn't exist anywhere
except in the mind.

DALE CARNEGIE

25 September

The past cannot be changed.
The future is yet in your power.

ANON

26 September

The way out is always through.

ROBERT FROST

27 September

God, give us the serenity to accept what cannot be changed; give us the courage to change what should be changed; give us the wisdom to distinguish one from the other.

REINHOLD NIEBUHR

28 September

Change will not come if we wait for some other person or some other time. We are the ones we've been waiting for. We are the change that we seek.

BARACK OBAMA

29 September

No one is so brave that he is not
disturbed by something unexpected.

JULIUS CAESAR

30 September

It does not do well to dwell on dreams and forget to live.

J.K. ROWLING

Conkers!

You know what's coming when you arrive at the month of October. The never-ending, halcyon days of summer are a thing of the past and will soon be replaced by dark early mornings and evenings when the clocks go back. I'm in two minds when it comes to this time of year, however. Autumn, in some respects, is a spectacular season, the last hurrah before the harsh chill of winter takes hold, a time to pull on your wellies and revel in all those vibrant purple, browny-yellow, orange and red colours. But I can also understand why autumn, especially in poetry, has often been seen as a gloomy or melancholy season. Even though we know the circle of life is ongoing, with spring and new birth on the way in due course, autumn is a time that makes us confront inevitable loss, decay and death.

The end of October approaches a season in the liturgical year when we remember saints, martyrs and all the faithfully departed (Christians celebrate All Saints' Day and All Souls' Day on 1 and 2 November, respectively). But I doubt this is why such a song and dance is now made about Halloween; it's become almost as commercial as Christmas. Where I live everyone seems to be embracing their spooky side more and more, with whole houses being decorated eerily. Last year my village was awash with trick or treaters of all ages dressed like extras from A *Nightmare on Elm Street*!

Looking back, there was something so special about the autumnal sun and crisp, clean air where I lived as a young boy in North Wales. This time of year offered up the perfect opportunity to go on a special hunt. Is there a greater joy than finding a huge, newly dropped conker? Well, yes of course there is, but try telling that to nine-year-old Aled – I was obsessed by them! They were as rare as hen's teeth where I lived and we would spend days, a bit like miniature truffle pigs, trying to sniff out a horse chestnut tree. If and when we found one, we had various techniques to get the prickly seeds down from the branches. Sticks would be thrown, usually to ill effect, until, eventually, one of us would be drafted into attempting the climb. This almost invariably resulted in someone rushing home with a suspected broken bone.

My love affair with the humble conker, which was far from fruitful, would change one fateful Sunday morning. My mum had dropped me off at Bangor Cathedral where I was a chorister, and I was walking through the cathedral gardens on my way to sing in the choral eucharist when an almighty gust of wind blew down what must have been at least fifty conkers. I was in heaven, furiously filling trouser and coat pockets with as many as I could hold. For me it was like winning the lottery. A divine moment on the way to another Divine Moment (for which I was already running late!).

As you will know, conkers aren't edible and, contrary to the advice of old wives' tales, they don't keep spiders out of your house if you strategically place them in room corners. So why, exactly, was I so obsessed with them? Granted, the fun of the hunt had something to do with it; but the main reason was to do with the noble sport itself. The game of conkers has two players, each with his or her own carefully selected conker, with a hole bored through it, on a string or shoelace. The basic idea of the game is to strike the opponent's conker and try to break it – your conker is then the winner and can count up its victories. Initially the conker is a 'none-er' and its first win makes it a 'one-er'; if it wins again, it takes a score of one for itself plus its opponents score to add to its own. For example, if an 'eight-er' beats a 'three-er', it scores one for the win, and takes the three from the vanquished opponent – so the victorious conker is now a 'twelve-er' (and something to be respected among your peers!).

In my school we also had a rule that if your opponent dropped his or her conker then you were within your rights to stamp on it, without doubt the cruellest way to lose. Cheating was part of the 'sport' because everyone wanted the hardest conker. So some were placed in vinegar, some were baked in the oven or painted with nail varnish – all to harden the fruit. I was once told by a farmer that the way to cultivate the perfect hard, unbeatable conker was to submerge it into cow dung. To this day I don't know if he had the winning formula as I didn't have the stomach to try it! So, each year I dried mine out in the airing cupboard and enjoyed very moderate success.

I remember a few years back getting equally excited about finding some conkers on a walk with my children. I explained the game and eagerly set about preparing for a match. I wasted my time, however; my son humoured me for about thirty minutes before going back to his iPad. How times have changed! And even though many believe that the game is dying out as a result of health and safety regulations (honestly!), I'm delighted that there is still one part of England taking it seriously. On the second Sunday of October each year the World

Conker Championships take place in the beautiful village of Southwick near Oundle in Northamptonshire. They've been going on since 1965 and draw competitors from all over the world to raise a shed load of money to help visually impaired people. Indeed the event is growing in popularity every year, with winners coming from as far afield as Mexico and Austria. So maybe I should come out of retirement and enter myself? I just need to find out where in central London I can source some of the Welsh farmer's conker-hardening magic formula!

1 October

Without rain nothing grows.
Learn to embrace the storms of your life.

ANON

2 October

Difficult roads often lead to
beautiful destinations.

ANON

3 October

We don't stop playing because we grow old;
we grow old because we stop playing.

GEORGE BERNARD SHAW

4 October

Ever tried. Ever failed. No matter.
Try again. Fail again. Fail better.

SAMUEL BECKETT

5 October

Find a place inside where there's joy,
and the joy will burn out the pain.

JOSEPH CAMPBELL

6 October

In three words I can sum up everything
I've learned about life: it goes on.

ROBERT FROST

7 October

We are all in the gutter, but some of us
are looking at the stars.

OSCAR WILDE

8 October

I can't change the direction of the wind,
but I can adjust my sails to always reach
my destination.

JIMMY DEAN

9 October

Truth is, everybody is going to hurt you; you just gotta find the ones worth suffering for.

BOB MARLEY

10 October

Plant seeds of kindness and watch your
blessings flow abundantly.

CHARMAINE J. FORDE

11 October

O God, creator of our land, our earth, the trees,
the animals and humans, all is for your honour.

The drums beat it out, and people sing about it,
and they dance with noisy joy that you are the Lord.

You also have pulled the other continents out of the sea.
What a wonderful world you have made out of wet mud,
and what beautiful men and women!
We thank you for all the beauty of this earth.

The grace of your creation is like a cool day between
    rainy seasons.
We drink in your creation with our eyes.
We listen to the bird's jubilee with our ears.

How strong and good and sure your earth smells,
and everything that grows there.

Be with us in our countries and in all Africa, and in the
    whole world.
Prepare us for the service that we should render.

ASHANTI PRAYER

12 October

Remember that not getting
what you want is sometimes
a wonderful stroke of luck.

DALAI LAMA

13 October

Our greatest weakness lies in giving up.
The most certain way to succeed is always
to try just one more time.

THOMAS EDISON

14 October

May the earth continue to live.
May the heavens above continue to live.
May the rains continue to dampen the land.
May the wet forests continue to grow.
Then the flowers shall bloom
And we people shall live again.

HAWAIIAN PRAYER

15 October

Never limit yourself because of others'
limited imagination; never limit others
because of your own limited imagination.

MAE JEMISON

16 October

Count your age by friends, not years.
Count your life by smiles, not tears.

JOHN LENNON

17 October

Slow but steady wins the race.

AESOP

18 October

I like living. I have sometimes been wildly, despairingly, acutely miserable, racked with sorrow, but through it all I still know quite certainly that just to be alive is a grand thing.

AGATHA CHRISTIE

19 October

Although the people living across the ocean
    surrounding us,
I believe, are all our brothers and sisters,
Why are there constant troubles in this world?
Why do winds and waves rise in the ocean
    surrounding us?
I only earnestly wish that the wind will soon puff
    away all the clouds
Which are hanging over the tops of the mountains.

SHINTO PRAYER

20 October

Treat the earth well.
It was not given to you by your parents,
It was loaned to you by your children.
We do not inherit the Earth from our Ancestors,
We borrow it from our Children.

ANCIENT INDIAN PROVERB

21 October

All of life is peaks and valleys. Don't let
the peaks get too high and the valleys too low.

JOHN WOODEN

22 October

A man is not finished when he is defeated.
He is finished when he quits.

RICHARD NIXON

23 October

Do not dwell in the past, do not
dream of the future, concentrate
the mind on the present moment.

BUDDHA

24 October

Life is an opportunity, benefit from it.
Life is beauty, admire it.
Life is a dream, realise it.
Life is a challenge, meet it.
Life is a duty, complete it.
Life is a game, play it.
Life is a promise, fulfil it.
Life is sorrow, overcome it.
Life is a song, sing it.
Life is a struggle, accept it.
Life is a tragedy, confront it.
Life is an adventure, dare it.
Life is luck, make it.
Life is too precious, do not destroy it.
Life is life, fight for it.

MOTHER TERESA

25 October

Very often a change of self is needed
more than a change of scene.

ARTHUR CHRISTOPHER BENSON

26 October

Though no one can go back and make
a brand new start, anyone can start from
now and make a brand new ending.

CARL BARD

27 October

When there is a hill to climb,
don't think that waiting will make it smaller.

ANON

28 October

Nothing gives one person so great
advantage over another, as to remain always
good and unruffled under the circumstances.

THOMAS JEFFERSON

29 October

Be still, my soul: the Lord is on thy side.
Bear patiently the cross of grief or pain.
Leave to thy God to order and provide;
In every change, he faithful will remain.
Be still, my soul: thy best, thy heavenly friend
Through thorny ways leads to a joyful end.

KATHERINE VON SCHLEGEL

30 October

There's only one corner of the universe you can
be certain of improving, and that's your own self.

ALDOUS HUXLEY

31 October

Short cuts make long delays.

J.R.R. TOLKIEN

Remembrance

Over the years, I have been involved in many Remembrance Day television programmes and events. It is always a very special privilege to give my services in memory of those who have done so much for us, and for our country. Most recently, I visited the wonderful Poppy Factory in Richmond upon Thames. It's a wonderful facility that has been supporting veterans with health conditions into civilian employment for nearly a hundred years. In that time, the Richmond factory has also been home to the Remembrance poppy. It's a fascinating place full of great people, and I thoroughly appreciated my visit, along with the opportunity to publicise their sterling work.

Throughout my career, I have sung at the Cenotaph and numerous services and concerts, to commemorate the fallen and give thanks to those who served and are serving our country now. I've even been lucky enough to sing a duet with the forces' sweetheart Dame Vera Lynn! As a broadcaster I have been as far afield as the Falkland Islands to film, when I spent two weeks there to make a programme about the 1982 Falklands War. I got to know some of the islanders and the armed forces stationed there. The Falklands are a couple of isolated and sparsely populated islands in the south-west Atlantic Ocean. We were based predominantly in the capital, Port Stanley, on the East Island. There's so much to see and do there, especially if you love history and wildlife. My one regret is that I didn't get to see a penguin.

One of my filming locations was on Mount Tumbledown, one of the highest points near the town of Port Stanley. On the night of 13–14 June 1982 the British launched an assault and succeeded in driving Argentinian forces from the mountain. It was a fierce, hard, night battle that was later dramatised in the BBC film *Tumbledown*. A cross had been set up in tribute to the soldiers who gave their lives in that place and we were due to film it. But the weather was so atrocious I found it difficult even to step out of the jeep I had travelled in up to Mount Tumbledown, let alone deliver any lines in situ. There was a sheeting cold wind and the hailstones hitting my face caused agony. I only managed the line, 'I'm struggling to stand here for seconds. God knows what it was like for the soldiers up here for hours!' I retreated back into the warm jeep and felt tremendous pride for our armed forces. That moment made me realise how lucky I was and how I should never take them for granted.

Back in 2019 I had the honour of interviewing the amazing ninety-three-year-old D-Day veteran Harry Billinge for a very special *Songs of Praise* which came from France, to mark seventy-five years since D-Day. Harry took me to the Bayeux War Cemetery and reflected on his faith and the sacrifices made in the Battle of Normandy. He was only eighteen at the time and landed on Gold Beach at 'H-Hour', 6.30 a.m., on 6 June 1944. Harry was a sapper with the Royal Engineers and was part of the first wave of troops. It was a very moving interview where he told me that he firmly believed that God had carried him through life for a purpose. He said he was delighted and honoured to do what he has done so tirelessly for so many years, which is to keep alive the memory of those who died in battle.

During the war he often prayed for his fellow soldiers and was tasked with keeping them positive. He poignantly told me that the guns of Alamance are now silent, but he hears them every day of his life. The time we spent together will forever be with me and I was overjoyed when he allowed me to use some of his words on a *Blessings* album I created (though I'm convinced his lovely wife talked him into it!). I love the way he passionately speaks from the heart in between the two songs 'If I can help somebody then my living has not been in vain' and 'Let there be peace on earth'. He is a true hero, a legend, and I was thrilled when he was awarded an MBE for raising thousands of pounds towards the cost of building a national memorial honouring his fallen comrades.

We have to remember and be thankful to those who gave their lives so we can live. Which brings me to another very different but hugely significant event that takes place across the pond commemorating the Founding Fathers of the United States. Thanksgiving is based on the colonial Pilgrims' 1621 harvest meal. A group of Europeans, who became known as the Pilgrims, had had trouble growing enough food to eat in preceding years. The Native Americans had taught the Pilgrims how to grow crops successfully and, to thank them for this, the Pilgrims invited them to a big feast.

The holiday continues to be an occasion for Americans to gather together for a day of family, feasting and football. The typical meal for Thanksgiving is similar in many ways to a traditional British Christmas dinner: turkey, bread stuffing, potatoes and cranberries, with the addition of some pumpkin pie on the menu. I was fortunate to be in New York for Thanksgiving once and got to witness the Thanksgiving Parade put on by the US department store Macy's. It's the world's largest parade and bigger and better than anything I've ever seen. There are marching bands, balloons, cheerleaders, floats and performers ranging from the up-and-coming to A-list celebrities. A word of advice though – don't go if you're no good in crowds!

And, finally, a little bit of trivia for you. There are, of course, fireworks galore to celebrate not only Bonfire Night but also Diwali in November, along with a few sparklers for Scottish chef Gordon Ramsay as he celebrates a birthday during the month. So if you are sitting down to a hearty Thanksgiving meal somewhere in the world, do remember those who gave of themselves in the past, and I sincerely hope there are no 'kitchen nightmares' during the culinary preparations!

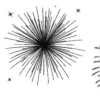

1 November

Do not go gentle into that good night.
Rage, rage against the dying of the light.

DYLAN THOMAS

2 November

The world breaks everyone,
and afterward, some are strong
at the broken places.

ERNEST HEMINGWAY

3 November

Old friends pass away, new
friends appear. It is just like the
days. An old day passes, a new day
arrives. The important thing is to
make it meaningful: a meaningful
friend – or a meaningful day.

DALAI LAMA

4 November

The weak can never forgive.
Forgiveness is the attribute of the strong.

MAHATMA GANDHI

5 November

Death is not the greatest loss in life. The greatest loss is what dies inside us while we live.

NORMAN COUSINS

6 November

That which does not kill us
makes us stronger.

FRIEDRICH NIETZSCHE

7 November

Insanity: doing the same thing over and over again and expecting different results.

ANON

8 November

Life is not always easy to live, but the opportunity to do so is a blessing beyond comprehension. In the process of living, we will face struggles, many of which will cause us to suffer and to experience pain.

L. LIONEL KENDRICK

9 November

However difficult life may seem, there is always something you can do and succeed at.

STEPHEN HAWKING

10 November

The truth is, we all face hardships of some kind, and you never know the struggles a person is going through. Behind every smile, there's a story of a personal struggle.

ADRIENNE C. MOORE

11 November

At the going down of the sun and
in the morning. We will remember them.

LAURENCE BINYON

12 November

Sometimes you will never know the value
of a moment, until it becomes a memory.

DR SEUSS

13 November

When we lose one blessing, another is
often most unexpectedly given in its place.

C.S. LEWIS

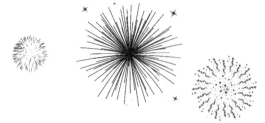

14 November

A life spent making mistakes is not only more honourable, but more useful than a life spent doing nothing.

GEORGE BERNARD SHAW

15 November

Life is 10% what happens to you
and 90% how you react to it.

CHARLES R. SWINDOLL

16 November

To err is human; to forgive, divine.

ALEXANDER POPE

17 November

Our business in this world is not to succeed,
but to continue to fail, in good spirits.

ROBERT LOUIS STEVENSON

18 November

Life is a gamble. You can get hurt, but people
die in plane crashes, lose their arms and legs
in car accidents; people die every day. Same
with fighters: some die, some get hurt, some
go on. You just don't let yourself believe it
will happen to you.

MUHAMMAD ALI

19 November

He who knows others is wise.
He who knows himself is enlightened.
He who conquers others has physical strength.
He who conquers himself is strong.

LAO TZU

20 November

When thinking about life, remember this:
no amount of guilt can change the past and no
amount of anxiety can change the future.

ANON

21 November

These are times in which a genius would wish to live. It is not in the still calm of life, or the repose of a pacific station, that great characters are formed . . . Great necessities call out great virtues.

ABIGAIL ADAMS

22 November

The soul would have no rainbow
if the eyes had no tears.

NATIVE AMERICAN PROVERB

23 November

Blessed are those who can give without remembering and take without forgetting.

BERNARD MELTZER

24 November

And once the storm is over, you won't remember how you made it through, how you managed to survive. You won't even be sure, in fact, whether the storm is really over. But one thing is certain. When you come out of the storm, you won't be the same person who walked in. That's what this storm's all about.

HARUKI MURAKAMI

25 November

Success always demands a greater effort.

WINSTON CHURCHILL

26 November

Be strong enough to stand alone,
smart enough to know when you need
help, and brave enough to ask for it.

ANON

27 November

Every great journey begins with one step and it begins with moving forward, turning on the engine, and shifting into the right gear at the right time. Remember, going through pain is temporary and it will subside, but quitting on the other hand lasts forever.

LOUIE HERRON

28 November

Tough times never last, but tough people do.

DR ROBERT SCHULLER

29 November

You cannot shake hands with a clenched fist.

INDIRA GANDHI

30 November

If you don't stand for something
you will fall for anything.

GORDON A. EADIE

The Most Wonderful Time of the Year

I realise that December for some can be a very lonely and upsetting time, but I hope that for most people Christmas is magical and deeply spiritual. It's a time to let bygones be bygones, to enjoy a few days off work and for families to come together in celebration of the gift of life – and for Christians that gift of life comes in the form of a special baby named Jesus, being born into the world to redeem us all.

For me it's my favourite time of year, without doubt. It's always ferociously busy, promoting a new record or singing glorious Christmas tunes in countless concerts up and down the country, in which I also recite poetry written to fill one and all with good cheer. Wasn't it crooner Andy Williams who reinforced, through song, that it's the most wonderful time of the year? Even if you don't get up to much mistletoeing (is that even a word?)!

I shall forever be associated with Christmas as a result of a song I sang as a child that depicted a young boy flying off with a snowman to see Father Christmas in a magical kingdom, full of balloons and teddy bears. You've probably seen the cartoon – it's on every year, after all. I should like to take this opportunity, once and for all, to put it out there that it's not my voice you hear on the aforementioned original film; I did the single that became a hit a few years after it was released. Please don't judge me. I've conned no one. I was fifteen, from North Wales, and did as I was told! The reason I was asked to record the song in the first place was that I was the boy soloist on the scene in those days. I'd released ten albums by the time I was asked to go into the studio to record *The Snowman*, which I thought was only going to be an advert for the superstore Toys 'R' Us; I'd only learned the thirty seconds needed for the ad! The recording session went quickly so I was asked to record the whole song and my undying gratitude goes to the person that suggested it – my kids are also very thankful!

Personally, the magic of Christmas is inextricably connected to festive music. My love affair (and it really is one) with carols started at primary school in North Wales where I remember, as if it were yesterday, singing 'Away in a Manger' sitting cross-legged on the uncomfortable, wooden floor of the tiny assembly hall, with the waft of lunch coming through the canteen shutters. It was magical! The perfect marriage of words and music hit me from the off. So simple, yet what a scene it conjured up:

The cattle are lowing, the baby awakes
But little Lord Jesus, no crying he makes.

I was hooked and transported to Bethlehem there and then. A wonderful carol linked with the most wonderful time of year. What's not to love? The power of these pieces cannot be underestimated, in my humble opinion, whether you're a Christian or not. The greatest carols seem to embody the enchantment that is in the air during this month.

My deep fondness for Christmas music was greatly enhanced when I became a chorister at Bangor Cathedral. Singing the ancient and modern carols in a very special place of worship, dear to my heart, in the run-up to my favourite time in the year was such a privilege. We, the choristers, could see the utter joy lighting up the faces of members of the congregation as they sang these tunes, and this unadulterated feeling of joy meant that, for a short time, problems were forgotten and all was good with the world. It felt as if there was a palpable magic in the air. Even now when I narrate a Christmas concert in a secular hall, and the throng is invited to join in a carol, these magical tunes, which are packed full of nostalgia for so many, have the ability to melt even the hardest of hearts. I remember looking into the audience a couple of years ago and seeing a big hairy biker (not from the TV I hasten to add) heartily singing 'Hark! The Herald Angels Sing' with eyes full of tears, the tune obviously bringing back years and years of memories.

It's also natural as we get to the end of the year to take stock, to take the foot off the pedal, reminisce and relive the good and the bad times. That's what I love about December: it gives us something to aim for, an end goal to achieve, if you like. Whether it's been a great, good or rather indifferent year, you get to December and you know the angels will be rejoicing at the birth of Jesus and, chances are, whether you believe or not, some spirit will be in you. And, as an added bonus, if you have been good, Santa will have a sack full of pressies. You may even get to build a snowman (I just had to go there!).

So, give yourself a pat on the back – you've made it to the end of another year, hopefully relatively unscathed. It's time to relax, give thanks, eat and drink too much, sing carols with gusto, play board games you wouldn't think of playing any other time of year and watch trash on the TV. And apologies in advance if I seem to be on television and radio more than usual this month. Take heart in the fact that, just like Santa, I'll be gone in January. But in the meantime, let's make merry and enjoy a very happy Christmas, the most wonderful time of the year!

1 December

A thousand words will not leave
so deep an impression as one deed.

HENRIK IBSEN

2 December

I survived because the fire inside me
burned brighter than the fire around me.

ANON

3 December

The important thing is not what they think
of me, but what I think of them.

QUEEN VICTORIA

4 December

It is impossible to live without failing at
something, unless you live so cautiously
that you might as well not have lived at all,
in which case you have failed by default.

J.K. ROWLING

5 December

No matter what your current circumstances
are, if you can imagine something better for
yourself, you can create it.

JOHN ASSARAF

6 December

You're only here for a short visit. Don't hurry, don't worry. And be sure to smell the flowers along the way.

WALTER HAGEN

7 December

To achieve great things, two things are needed: a plan, and not quite enough time.

LEONARD BERNSTEIN

8 December

If you want something you never had,
you have to do something you've never done.

9 December

To see a world in a grain of sand
And a heaven in a wild flower,
Hold infinity in the palm of your hand
And eternity in an hour.

WILLIAM BLAKE

10 December

There is only one thing in the world worse than being talked about, and that is not being talked about.

OSCAR WILDE

11 December

You know what charm is: a way of getting the answer yes without having asked any clear question.

ALBERT CAMUS

12 December

It's not what happens to you, but how you react to it that matters.

EPICTETUS

13 December

That which we are, we are;
One equal temper of heroic hearts,
Made weak by time and fate, but strong in will
To strive, to seek, to find, and not to yield.

ALFRED, LORD TENNYSON

14 December

To be so strong that nothing
Can disturb your peace of mind.
To talk health, happiness, and prosperity
To every person you meet.

To make all your friends feel
That there is something in them.
To look at the sunny side of everything
And make your optimism come true.

To think only the best, to work only for the best,
And to expect only the best.
To be just as enthusiastic about the success of others
As you are about your own.

To forget the mistakes of the past
And press on to the greater achievements of the future.
To wear a cheerful countenance at all times
And give every living creature you meet a smile.

To give so much time to the improvement of yourself
That you have no time to criticize others.
To be too large for worry, too noble for anger, too strong
    for fear,
And too happy to permit the presence of trouble.

To think well of yourself and to proclaim this fact to the
    world,
Not in loud words but great deeds.
To live in faith that the whole world is on your side
So long as you are true to the best that is in you.

CHRISTIAN D. LARSON

15 December

What I do today is important
because I am exchanging a day
of my life for it.

ANON

16 December

Trust yourself. You know more than you think you do.

DR BENJAMIN SPOCK

17 December

I've seen better days, but I've also seen worse. I don't have everything that I want, but I do have all I need. I woke up with some aches and pains, but I woke up. My life may not be perfect, but I am blessed.

ANON

18 December

For all sad words of tongue and pen,
the saddest are these: 'It might have been'.

JOHN GREENLEAF WHITTIER

19 December

Someday, everything will make perfect sense.
So for now, laugh at the confusion, smile
through the tears, and keep reminding
yourself that everything happens for a reason.

JOHN MAYER

20 December

In the depths of winter,
I finally learned there was in
me an invincible summer.

ALBERT CAMUS

21 December

Never look backwards or you'll fall down
the stairs.

RUDYARD KIPLING

22 December

Christmas is most truly Christmas when
we celebrate it by giving the light of love
to those who need it most.

RUTH CARTER STAPLETON

23 December

What is Christmas?
It is tenderness for the past,
Courage for the present,
Hope for the future.

AGNES M. PAHRO

24 December

'Twas the night before Christmas,
when all through the house,
not a creature was stirring,
not even a mouse.
The stockings were hung by the chimney with care,
In hopes that St Nicholas soon would be there.

CLEMENT CLARKE MOORE

25 December

One of the most glorious messes in the world is the mess created in the living room on Christmas Day. Don't clean it up too quickly.

ANDY ROONEY

26 December

We are better throughout the year for
having, in spirit, become a child again at
Christmas time.

LAURA INGALLS WILDER

27 December

The truth is that someone somewhere is always
dealing with something bigger, more tragic and more
heart-wrenching than we are, and it takes a rude
awakening for us to realise how blessed we truly are.

PAUL BARRATT

28 December

The best of all gifts around any
Christmas tree: the presence of a happy
family all wrapped up in each other.

BURTON HILLIS

29 December

Never look back unless you're planning
to go that way.

HENRY DAVID THOREAU

30 December

I like the dreams of the future
better than the history of the past.

THOMAS JEFFERSON

31 December

When all the dust is settled and all the crowds are gone, the things that matter are faith, family, and friends.

BARBARA BUSH

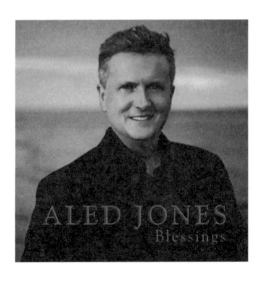

Accompanying the release of *Everyday Blessings*
is Aled's 40th album *Blessings*, featuring duets with
Dame Judi Dench, Sami Yusuf and D-Day veteran Harry
Billinge MBE. At the heart of the album is Aled's firm
belief that peace, love and kindness are at the core
of all faiths – these are the values that bind us
together and come to us in times of need.

'I hope this album offers a moment out from
the uncertainty and stress of the world around us at the
moment. Whether you subscribe to a faith or not this
album is a chance to escape somewhere else and
focus on the positive in all our lives.'

Aled Jones

HODDER &
STOUGHTON

Hodder & Stoughton is the UK's
leading Christian publisher,
with a wide range of books from
the bestselling authors in the UK
and around the world ranging from
Christian lifestyle and theology to
apologetics, testimony and fiction.
We also publish the world's
most popular Bible translation
in modern English, the New
International Version, renowned
for its accuracy and readability.

Hodderfaith.com   Hodderbibles.co.uk
@HodderFaith   /HodderFaith